29/24    £3
LMCC
PHIL.

KU-114-097

# LIFE'S CURRENCY

# LIFE'S CURRENCY

Time, Money & Energy
an anthology of shorter writings of

## WINIFRED RUSHFORTH

OBE, MB, ChB
(1885–1983)

Gateway Books, Bath
and Interbook Inc, San Leandro, Calif.

First published in 1985 by
GATEWAY BOOKS
19 Circus Place,
Bath BAI 2PW

in the U.S.A. by
INTERBOOK Inc,
14895 E.14th Street,
San Leandro, CA 94577

British Library Cataloguing in Publication Data:
Rushforth, Winifred
    Life's Currency: time money and energy.
    1. Psychology - Religious aspects - Christianity
    I. Title
    261.5'15    BF51

ISBN 0-946551-19-7

Set in Sabon 10½ on 11
by Mathematical Composition Setters Ltd.,
Salisbury, Wilts
Printed and bound in Great Britain
by Photobooks of Bristol
and Paperback Binders (Oxford), Abingdon

# Contents

# Contents

# Editors' Introduction

Winifred Rushforth was a legend in her native Scotland, but she also attracted people from all over the world who came to seek her help with their problems or to find some inspiration. For she was a very original kind of therapist – positive, enthusiastic, definitely charismatic, passionately keen on helping the person to realise his true potential talents. Sir Laurens van der Post once asked her the secret of her extraordinary energy – until the very end of her life, aged 98, she ran six groups a week and saw several patients a day – and she replied "I never go against my unconscious".

A Scottish audience was built up through her religious broadcasts she could make the Christian teaching come alive through reinterpretation of some of the great stories of the Bible with modern psychological insights. A wider audience came with her television appearance on the BBC "Friends" series with her daughter, Dr. Diana Bates, but the response to the Leslie Smith Radio 4 interview was immense. We are very grateful for his permission to reproduce this at the end of the book.

Dr. Rushforth was undoubtedly aware that her personality came over well when she talked. In many ways she was a very practical person rather than a book writer. Though she wrote many articles, she had reservations about her ability to write a book. Her first, a short one *The Outstretched Finger*, published in 1933, on understanding the child's and the family's needs, now seems somewhat dated. It had been written before she had had her personal analysis. During the many years that followed when she was Medical Director of the Davidson Clinic, the pioneering centre for family therapy in Edinburgh, she contributed a large number of articles for the Davidson Clinic Bulletin between 1946 and 1968, some of which are reproduced here.

During the late 1960s, in response to many promptings from her friends and grateful patients, she made some faltering steps towards a book on the importance of the unconscious processes in our lives. Dr. Rushforth had difficulties in seeing the book as a whole, in standing back from the themes in which she was so passionately engaged. She was quite sceptical about its value, right up to its final publication in 1980.

So when an enthusiastic response came from all over the world to *Something is Happening*, it clearly delighted her. The book brought a spiritual awareness and understanding to individual psychological processes, meeting a need that many people felt. It has a message that spreads by word of mouth rather than by advertising or marketing, and it has been through four printings in five years.

Many of the patients of whom Dr. Rushforth had asked "tell me your story" turned the request back to her. So, her confidence built up with the success of *Something is Happening*, she enthusiastically turned to her autobiography. She finished it in the year of her death and it was published the following year, 1984. Concurrently with this last work, she was planning a sequel to *Something is Happening* on the theme of potentiality, one of her favourite topics. This became a partial draft for "God's Currency", about the challenge we all face to make the best use of our individual talents of time, energy and money, and it forms the first part of the present volume.

Rather than attempt to weave together a sequel to *Something is Happening* we decided to make this a retrospective collection of shorter pieces of Dr. Rushforth's writing. The articles were written over thirty-six years; some have appeared in "The Bulletin" or other magazines. About half have not been published before. We have grouped them under five appropriate headings.

Dr. Rushforth became partially blind in the last two years of her life, which meant that she was dependent on the help of a friend for reading and writing. As a result some of the articles inevitably became loose in their structure, and these, by modest editorial intervention, have been made more manageable. In a collection such as this some repetition is inevitable; the main messages are often restated, arising from different starting points, but we feel this serves to indicate how strongly Dr. Rushforth felt that certain topics needed to be more widely talked about and understood.

Winifred Rushforth found great comfort and inspiration from poetry. We have therefore included some of her favourite quotations to make this anthology more personal.

*Life's Currency* is published to celebrate the 100th anniversary of Winifred Rushforth's birth, on 21st August, 1885, and to coincide with an exhibition which the City Art Centre is mounting as a centenary tribute to one of Edinburgh's pioneering daughters.

# Thank You God

I break off this morning from the personal story of "How I began" to write again about the analytical situation. This change is determined by two happenings. After I had left my morning's task I opened a letter from a patient who used to come to me in the 1930's. Her letter ended by saying that she had heard I was writing a book. "Please write it for your patients, *not* for the other analysts." This was the occasion for the words "Thank you, God" which I am in the habit of using when something very pleasant or very apposite occurs. My early morning coffee out of the bedside thermos may be just the right strength and temperature – "Thank you, God." The dying moon may be shining into my eastern window as I go to bed or the lovely morning star in the heavens as I wake before sunrise – "Thank you, God". A child in the painting studio looks over my shoulder and says "I like your picture" – "Thank you, God". Indeed now this morning as I tended my plants in the window I find that my fuchsia has budded again, the fourth time since June when Helen gave it to me. Yes, indeed, "Thank you, God." I was so sad when its first lovely flowers scattered but the realisation that again and again it would blossom if I cared for it aright, brought me great pleasure and thankfulness.

But this digression occurred because of the sudden insight Gwen's letter brought "*not for the other analysts*". I see that I have delayed writing because of these professional workers whom I must have pictured as 'siblings' in the psychiatric world, and therefore I feared their criticism and the anger and contempt I might arouse in them if I produced a book about analysis. I remembered that to my brothers I was 'only a girl' unlikely to produce anything of value, to the straight psychiatrists a nobody, and to the analysts of the Freudian and Jungian schools who was I? Had I undergone the long training analysis demanded by the orthodox? Where were my credentials? I could almost hear the school-girl expression, "What a cheek!" Well now, today, I understand. This writing is *not* for analysts; they have read all the books; they have attended all the lectures; they know all that is appropriate for orthodox treatment. Not for them my book so "Thank you God". I fish out the last letter I had from a possible publisher, dated two years back. He said, "Perhaps I should emphasise once again that we are primarily a publisher of books for the general public, and it is no use pretending that we can publish books of too technical a nature. . . but I do realise that there is a vast public interest in the sort of work which your clinic does and I do believe that a fairly popular account of this would be of wide appeal, particularly if linked closely with your own life story".

The second thing that sent me back to the anlaytic aspect was that I 'happened' to listen to a schools' broadcast called "Involvement", with the sub-heading "Call no man an island" from one of the wonderful passages in literature dealing with what Jung in this century was to call "The Collective Unconscious".

*No man an island.* Am I indeed involved in a process of infinite complexity, we call it Evolution, now, in mankind, the evolution of consciousness? Since it was published in 1959 Teilhard de Chardin's book *The Phenomenon of Man* has mattered very much to me. I have read and re-read it. Each time it makes more sense, and I can link its teaching with the processes of analysis which are the obvious present-day techniques of bringing unconscious processes into consciousness. Faith I consider to be an aperture, a hole in the wall, between the dark world of the Unknown and Unknowing which lives our lives if we are unaware, and the Conscious life where the jig-saw pieces are laid on the table, we can handle them, make our-selves aware of the pattern, decide on their position in the picture, although this indeed is pre-determined. There *is* a picture. Our task is to restore what was destroyed when a machine was set to work to break it into the puzzle-pieces: now we re-create the picture.

Any long deep analysis brings this analogy of the jig-saw puzzle very frequently to mind. An image may recur in the dream without apparent significance; it is laid on one side but not forgotten until one day it supplies the needed link that makes further development possible.

I remember one such instance. A patient came to consult me rather against his better judgment, only because his headaches were becoming unbearable and his conduct causing surprise to himself no less than to his friends. He resented being questioned but was willing to recount his dreams as long as I didn't interpret them. At the first interview I asked him about his family situation in childhood. His parents had survived until he was adult. He had one sister about three years younger than himself "but," he said, "we can put her out of the picture. I see nothing of her and she was of no importance at any time of my life". A day or two later he told me of a dream in which his sister was leaning up against the radiator of his car. It could not be started until they got a *crane* to remove her! As we worked out *his* jig-saw we found that large important areas of his early life were concerned with her birth and the painful period when he was an ex-baby subject to night terrors and other distresses. But what was so fascinating was that towards the end of his analysis the *crane* had to be fitted into the picture. It was a Meccano crane belonging to the sixth and seventh years of his life when the brother-sister relationship gives rise to phantasies of marriage and reproduction, the sister taking the place of the mother in the Oedipus situation.

So now it is clear that this book is not competing with books about the technique of analysis, nor is it indeed written with any specific aim, but rather because it is fun to share insights and fun, too, that my travels in the dark continent of the Unconscious have shown me strange things and have cast light on many puzzles which each of us encounters in daily life.

*(1967)*

I am the vessel. The draught is God's.
And God is the thirsty one.

# God's Currency

I find it curious and interesting that I seem to have a compulsive desire to write about the 'currency' of time, money and energy. Our lives as human beings are greatly conditioned and influenced by these elements. Not only by how much, in each case, we have at our disposal but rather what use we make of them as the days pass to become a lifetime. We may well recognise ourselves as vehicles to carry them, 'Time at my disposal', similarly with money and energy. Each of them we take, we hold and we give again. We accept, we carry, and we dispense. Those of us who watch our dreams and the dreams of others know that vehicles of diverse kinds come to us as as symbols in our dreaming – every sort of carriage from a perambulator to a hearse. At the present time the vehicle is usually a motor car; often the vintage rather than the make is notable. Does the dreamer drive this car or is he driven by another? To be aware of the answer to this question may shed light on the responsibility we are taking for our own life. Are we at the wheel or is father, mother, husband, wife, or some other person in the driving seat?

It is good to know ourselves as vehicles, but how do we ourselves carry these three values? Are we burdened by them too much? They are embarrassing gifts and weigh on our shoulders. Possibly the vehicle is empty, at a standstill, unemployed, awaiting 'that' which will bring it into action and indicate a goal. Can we see ourselves rather as cheerful, willing drivers, picking up the loads and delivering them again, meeting the inevitable problems with spontaneity and resource, one with all the others used by the Guiding Power of all life to discover and attain the goal?

Time, money, energy: are they like hitch-hikers standing by the roadside awaiting a lift, hoping that some vehicle will pick them up so that they will move on and be taken on their journey, become current? Time stretches into infinity. Money that children used to treasure as pence is squandered by the nations. And energy? Cosmic in its source, it must be used. Only when it moves things does it fulfil its purpose and become a known reality. Poverty or riches? Scarcity or plenty? A trickle or a full river? What matters is that it keeps flowing, maintains its availability. A cup of cold water may save a man's life, while a torrent may destroy him.

Notice that the symbolism of currency can change from vehicle to channel. The former involves man's will and co-operation,the latter his passivity. In both are movement and currency; each was created to serve a purpose. Stasis and immobility bring death in their train, while movement, flow, libido are conducive to that 'life more abundant' towards which humanity is stretching.

A friend, perhaps a member of the family comes in to visit you and asks 'Anything I can do for you today? 'Well can you spare me some *time*?' 'Yes, sit down' 'I would like you to listen, I have something I want to talk about.' Or again the response might be 'Have you any cash to spare? I am temporarily hard up, my purse is empty'. Another might be 'Are you feeling energetic? A job is needing to be done for which I don't feel strong enough'. Time to spare, money to spare, energy to spare. What do we need today? What can we supply? What is current between us? What is needed by one is available from the other. Can you spare? Can we share?

John and Jenny have been married for some time. He has always given her an allowance and is rather cross when she exceeds the amount. She does not know what his total income is nor how he spends it: it may be accumulating in the bank but it is not *available* for her needs. Jim and Janet have quite a different way of managing their money matters. They have a joint account at the bank and when they go shopping or have an outing he likes to take out his wallet and quite obviously gets pleasure from the sharing. It seems curious that when this good feeling is so simply generated, the strain and tension of non-sharing cannot be abandoned. The Parable of the Talents in the Gospel is of course dealing with this, urging us to be conscious that money (and all other gifts) when used creatively and put into circulation greatly increase in value; but there is something more, an over-plus, expressed in the story as "Enter into the joy of the Lord". Jim and Janet obviously live a much more cheerful existence than John and Jenny where tension and difficult grudging attitudes are not conducive to a happy atmosphere.

When I had thought about Time, Money and Energy as being forms of currency, I began to see that men and women are also forms of currency. Perhaps we are 'God's Currency'? Availability, we found, was the testing word. Is cash available? Have you time to spare or have you any available time to give? And energy? Is it available now for that job awaiting completion, or are you too tired at present? An aquaintance of mine was recently recommended by her family physician to a psychiatrist, since she was greatly in need of help for an acute anxiety condition. She was given promise of a consultation in five weeks time, and it does not take much imagination to see how the anxiety would increase during the waiting period. Fortunately there are psychotherapists who don't work with this, but are aware that if anxious folk need help it is best to assume that they need it *now*, and they find ways of making themselves *available* at short notice for people in need.

Our curiosity gets to work: Why? Why have some people such a long waiting list and why can others find time? Are people in the first category more important, wiser, better qualifed or in any way superior to others who are on the spot for the sufferer? We do have the analogy of finding ourselves saying 'I have no time now; come back in five weeks time'; or with money perhaps 'I expect to receive a bonus next month, come back and some may be available'. Energy? We might conceivably give the answer 'I expect I shall feel stronger next week, next month, next year, try me later'.

None of these are aware of the urgent need. It may well be a here-and-now situation and the responses give no certainty that the future has the answer. We may well ask ourselves to which of these categories we belong. One way of life is to be increasingly aware of the value of the present moment and to train ourselves to work as closely as possible to the now. 'Do it now' and we find that immediate action is economical! The affair is over and dealt with, occupying a shorter time than would have been needed to plan it in the future. Yes, they taught us when were children 'Procrastination is the thief of time'. We might have grasped the truth better had it been put into simpler words, perhaps just 'Do it now as a good habit, it saves time'.

What do we achieve by procrastination? Attempts to create the image of a Very Important Person, and it tends to succeed: 'Dr so-and-so has become so famous that his waiting list is six weeks long'. I dont think Dr so-and-so would appreciate it if you or I said 'Something wrong here' and suggested ways out of the problem, but perhaps he may himself think about it and come to find other ways of doing his work, *now*.

# Time

Time, money, energy – none of these is easy to define. Time, so the dictionary says, is a period between two events – but, time and period have almost the same meaning. Time is a man-made conception and, if we follow the dream processes, we become aware that there is no time in the unconscious. Infancy and old age are linked, strangely, in the same incident, Today, more than ever, with the high cost of labour, we hear the words 'time is money'. Time is irrevocable, it cannot be stored. We know this is also true of electricity, which is a symbol of energy.

We say that really busy people always have time, they can make time – this indicates their creativity. Time now serves them, it is no longer their master. When we hear the words 'I have no time, I cannot make time', we must beware of negativity, that these people are not yet making full use of what is seeking its way in their lives.

Let us look, for a moment, at ways in which we think and speak of time. There are,for instance, some words that are common to the concepts of time, money and energy, and some of them go in opposites.

| | | |
|---|---|---|
| using time | – | wasting time |
| taking time | – | giving time |
| spending time | – | saving time |
| plenty of time | – | time is scarce |
| generous with time | – | grudging of time |
| finding time | – | losing time |
| wise about time | – | foolish about time |
| profligate with time | – | miserly with time |

These equally apply to money and energy.

The source of the gift is important with all three. In a real sense we are given time, given a life-time, and also given the moment, the 'now', which we sometimes call 'the only time we have'. Money, too, is to be earned, and the source of riches is labour. Energy is cosmic in its source, but it must be channelled through living creatures.

Do we sometimes feel our time is stolen – do we allow people to steal our time? An impertinence! Time is precious and, in old age, I testify that each day, each hour, seems to increase in value, becoming even more prized towards the latter end of life. But all through infancy, childhood, and adolescence, those of us who observe what is happening may well become aware of the unique opportunity of each stage in life through which the individual is passing. Adolescence, so often a time of rebellion against parents and against society, is also, we must remember, a time of great opportunity, and it soon passes as we settle down into adult life. In infancy and childhood the days are incredibly long but, as we grow older, we are often astonished at the acceleration that takes place, so that one Christmas time gives way to another Christmas time with surprising speed. In passing, let us just notice the curious phrase 'to run out of time'. Does this denote loss of creativity?

Sometimes it is important to consider what proportion of our life is spent in sleep. Some babies sleep almost continuously and we are told that much of this is used in dreaming. It is also said that, as age advances, less sleep is necessary and those people who carry heavy responsibilities are able to use a minimum. Napoleon and Winston Churchill are often quoted for their ability to minimise the amount of sleep they needed. Scientists tell us that three hours out of the twenty-four are essential for restoration of the physical frame. This amount of slumber, however, can be tolerated for only limited periods, but it is possible to habituate oneself to a five-hour sleep regime. Eight hours, which is considered normal in adult life, consumes a third of the available working day, and one third of one's total lifetime.

From personal observation, I would suggest that the practice of meditation, with attention to the breathing, shortens the time necessary for sleep. Many unfortunate people, troubled with insomnia, find themselves victims of negative suggestion such as, 'I shall be of no use tomorrow since I have had such a bad night'. Notice the words – 'bad night'. The practice of meditation may well enable us to think instead of a 'good night' with the gift of renewed energy for the day to follow. Auto-suggestion operates very efficiently during those drowsy non-sleeping hours, so let us beware, I would emphasise, of using negative attitudes, anticipating, perhaps, lack of energy.

This must stimulate us to think again about the source of energy. The psalmist's oft-quoted words found on tombstones – 'He giveth His beloved, sleep.' It is necessary to remind ourselves that there are two phases in this period of unconsciousness, indicated by brainwave activity which can be monitored; they are dreamless and dream-bearing sleep. From laboratory research, we learn that dreaming occurs in normal people, on an average, four times each night. On waking we so often know that we have been dreaming but the contents elude us and, frequently,we seem to cease from dreaming for many nights on end. There are also, of course, vivid dreams that cannot be forgotten. It is amusing to think how Joseph and the Egyptian butler and baker who Joseph met in prison, and Pharoah himself, are remembered in history as the dreamers of dreams.

## Time as currency

I find it strange today that I forget what you said to me yesterday, yet I clearly remember what one of my brothers said to me in my childhood "It is vulgar to be in a hurry". Later in life when the wisdom of the West Highland people stimulated my thought-processes I learned that when God created time He made plenty of it. My mother was fond of saying that the busiest people are the ones who can always find time for their friends, so the words 'Find time', 'Make time', 'Take time' come easily enough to me when the day is busy.

Just as we learn that money-wise currency is the cash in your purse or pocket, the coins available for immediate use, not locked away in a banking account – so too the availability of our time for the needs of others is a measure of our usefulness to mankind.

Take, hold, give, are words that have meaning in awareness of our breathing. Can we train ourselves to be mindful of the taking, holding, giving of breath – air, life-giving oxygen without which life cannot be sustained? Breath, we are told by Hebrew scholars, is, in their language, *ruach* which also means wind, spirit and life. We recollect the words of Christ "The wind bloweth where it listeth". It is invisible, inapprehensible yet it impinges upon us "such is...the spirit". *Spiro* I breath, and whatever our occupation with life's business we must *take time* to breathe, always enough time for the necessity. Such a realization would free us from much anxiety in the awareness of the *Now*, the given moment in which we act, looking neither with regret to past time nor with dread to what lies ahead. 'Do it now', use the current moment, and another strand in the pattern of your life has been woven in. The habitual use of the present moment 'do it now' is establishing the growth of the cloth without the off-putting delay of a tomorrow that may never come.

I suppose we all know people who are hard-pressed for time. We hear them say that they could be doing with another hour added to the twenty-four. That, however, is the given quota, and I believe that to make full use of it we must become more aware, more conscious, more mindful of how we are using it. How many hours out of the twenty-four for instance do we sleep? Does it amount to a third of our available time? Eight hours out of the twenty-four? By rising one hour earlier than usual I find the day becomes strangely more spacious. How important are holidays in frequency and duration?

To establish a rhythm between work and rest, effort and relaxation seems essential, but there is a way of life where the beating heart, the breathing body ask us to heed their lesson. The heart systole, its contraction, is inevitably and constantly followed by diastole, the dilation, so that throughout a life time the heart never takes a holiday. It rests, of course, and the resting is of equal importance to the working, but its nature in to integrate activity with passivity. Perhaps life is given to us to learn something of this balance, We are rested with a good night's sleep, with long holidays, but what about unemployment?

Looking ahead to retiring from work we anticipate a time of pleasure. All too often it becomes a time of boredom and we would gladly have work again since "now time hangs so heavily on our hands". No one is to be more envied than the creative man or woman to whom time is opportunity, who can find time for work, make time for friendship, who is aware of its value but aware too that a time will come when he will pass into the shadows and all that seems so important today, in present time will be forgotten. Will we leave footprints on the sands of time? Can we hope for a land of greater scope where the work that here is well begun will be complete and not undone? We must be, it seems, content with the time that is on our hands today, using it to work or to rest, we cannot yet see the pattern.

And what about the Sabbath, the seventh day? What about the sabbatical year in which the land must lie fallow? The Gospel teaching makes ridiculous the rigidity of the Jewish observation "The Sabbath is made for man and not man for the Sabbath". But the Sabbath is "the Lord's Day" and the wisdom of past ages tells us that the hurry of present life is not only undignified but harmful. We should be more aware of the rhythm of summer and winter, of night and day, of distraction and attraction, frustration and fulfilment. And so life-patterns when they are liberated, set free from compulsive rigid behaviour can take on a freedom of choice, a wisdom in making decisions that greatly adds to the joy of life. Can we wake up and realise what fun it is to be alive?

Let us remember again the words of our wise Scots poet William Dunbar who wrote –

Ah Freedom is noble thing
Freedom maks man to have lyking

It makes us enjoy life to know that life can be fun. We learn that Time need not dominate our lives, but as we gain wisdom and maturity we learn more about precious Time and our relationship to it.

## Leisure

*"Man's work ends with the sun. Women's work is never done"*

"If only I had time" all of us have complained at some time. We have also heard a wise person counter: "Nonsense, you have all the time there is." That too must be true, but how are we to find it? Why is this leisure so plentiful in some lives and so scarce in ours? Is there a resource upon which we can draw? Can anyone tell us the secret of finding leisure in the busiest life, of *making* time?

The fact is that we do all of us find leisure daily, for which of us does without sleep? Nature sees to it that all her children cease from their labour howeve hard they may have to work. We have in the living body with its beating heart a wonderful example of activity alternating with rest. All of life is rhythmic and we must all find leisure for growth to balance the effort of living.

Some can find leisure as the heart does, moment by moment relaxing. Others steal a few minutes in the hour, some steal an hour from the night when they can be alone. An autobiography published recently in America told of a man with a great urge to be an author but he had *no time* – long days of work involving much travelling in bus and train. One day he suddenly realised that he *had time* – the minutes and hours he spent in travel. He equipped himself with pen and notebook and made a beginning; soon he was publishing his books.

During the war we had specially trained commandos, the account of whose training sometimes came over the wireless. One such story was that after marching all day these boys had to run the last mile home. If the boys could do this perhaps their mothers had been too protective. What about an hour of different activity before bedtime? The commandos were trained to disregard fatigue. On what resources were they drawing? Is this training to avoid fatigue only a fantasy? "Even the youths shall faint and be weary and the young men shall utterly fall *but* they that wait upon the Lord shall renew their strength, they shall mount up on wings as eagles, they shall run and not be weary, they shall walk and not faint." Can we make this waiting on the Lord a reality so that we realise this great resource, then we shall have leisure and may set about thinking how best to use it.

You and I may have quite different ideas of how we would like to use our leisure. Mankind and womankind may even be divided into three classes if we watch them confronted with a spare hour. The first lot will want to find other people to talk to. Typically one would see them seating themselves round a table with others, eating and drinking, glad always to be in company, happier when they have food and drink to share. *Secondly* we would find a group who are indifferent to the others who must go and *do* something – walk a mile, or play some game or get down with a scrubbing brush, bodily activity is their idea of leisure. *Thirdly* the people who detach themselves from the others. Their idea of happiness is to be alone and probably to read or rest or merely to sit or lie and think in seclusion.

Since human beings are so different, some of them longing for noise and company, others only for stillness and quiet, it is obvious that we can lay down no laws other than to say that leisure is a deep necessity and must be discovered and used. If not used creatively boredom ensues, possibly resulting in ill-health of body and mind. The compulsive activities such as gambling, alcoholism, over-eating develop when we have 'nothing better to do'. Leisure on the other hand is re-creative in its nature and I would like to suggest some important aspects of it common to all.

Anxiety and leisure are not compatible – anxious folk don't know how to use their leisure. A patient once came to me suffering from a tired heart and nightmares. Her doctor said her heart would recover if I could do something about her bad dreams. I found she was very much afraid of life and also of death. She was the Company Secretary of a big business but she spent most of her day typing although the management provided her with a typist. She always took work home with her and, in case she might ever be idle, she also undertook the typing for a society to which she belonged. No leisure. Tap tap tap early morning until late at night.

At our Clinic we taught her to relax, to weave and to paint. She went back to work, and found that a typist could relieve her of most of her work. Then she found she had *leisure* to get into contact with the people amongst whom her life was spent. She made many new friends. She had leisure to paint and to weave and to introduce others to these activites. Her whole life became creative and lovely, her environment beautiful, and friends sprang up everywhere.

This all happened through a lessening of anxiety. It illustrates the words I have quoted elsewhere recorded in St. Paul's letter to Timothy, "God hath not given us the spirit of Fear (anxiety) but of power (energy) of love (good relationship) and of a sound mind (adjusted personality or tranquillity.) When we use tranquillizing drugs we may be less aware of our anxieties but less aware also of the highlights of feeling that make life good. They do not set free the creative impulses that are our birthright. This woman's life showed how anxiety destroys leisure and how in freedom from anxiety leisure becomes creative.

I can think of some interesting and important uses of leisure:-

I    Relaxation – quietness – awareness of one's own life – learning to Practise the Presence of God, meditation. 'No time' is a great excuse for not finding stillnesss or meditating. It *need* take no time but be slipped in to the moments. Jesus taught us that we need go neither to the temple nor to the mountains, but that the Father seeks us to worship Him in Spirit. This is the Here and Now of life, making use of the present moment which, after all, is the only one we possess.

II    To develop better relationships with others. 'No time' is a great barrier to friendship. To sit quietly and *listen* may be difficult for some of us but if we can relax and are quiet and acceptant we can find healing for ourselves as well as giving it to others by quiet listening. Through this, understanding comes between us and our neighbour, initiating acceptance of the many-sidedness of life and so enriching experience.

III    Creative leisure may be wisely used in activity of some sort or another. It may be of the nature of music (particularly free expression rather than listening.) Use of colour (painting, embroidery, weaving), the use of pencil to draw or pen to write. Craft work of every kind, wood, stone, clay and many other materials await the use of our hands and our imagination. Let us all try to obey the urge and begin; no-one knows the end nor how the gift may come to fruition.

IV    Drama – (which we call projection-activity) – through it feelings can be brought out instead of hurting within. Folk dancing, community singing, verse speaking are all useful in the same way. There is a great future in the use of drama in school life, in community experience, re-introducing traditions practised by our forebears.

V    Sport, athletics – bodily activity are of importance to sedentary workers especially in youth, but we need to be reminded of their value. It is so obvious that young people need to become aware of what their bodies can do. Young folk may well be taught that to keep their bodies healthy and strong is also a form of worship, as the body is the temple of the spirit. Yoga, recognizing this, is more than physical exercise. Tai-chi introduced from China is a rhythmic activity of great beauty – one of many available at the present time as we become open to learning from our neighbours.

I would like to emphasise and reiterate my belief that the wise use of leisure is of priceless value for growth and development of our human potential. on the other hand, to deny ourselves this gap in activity or to let it become boringly uncreative, is destructive and can only lead us back into unhappiness and desolation.

## Energy as Currency

Currency in terms of money is *what we have in our purses or pockets for spending* as distinct from the money safely invested or recorded in a bank account. It has to do with *availability*: Put your hand into your pocket, open your purse. Quite frequently we are surprised. Thinking we are out of cash we find a few coins or even a £10 note that is just what we needed and we say 'It was there all the time'.

And so with energy. Returning from work on a long summer's day an indignant husband has no energy to mow the lawn at his wife's request but surprisingly, a friend rings up suggesting a game of golf and the fatigue and self-pity disappear – there is plenty of energy and it must have been there all the time!

So strangely, energy defies definition; we are aware of it only in action, we can see what it does. By a subtle process known as auto-suggestion we find ourselves anticipating action or even emotion in advance and in so doing we may allow our energy to have little relationship with reality. Facing the prospect of a surgical operation, an X ray examination or a few days off work on doctor's orders we may find ourselves the victims of totally non-existent disease. In such circumstances we are wasting energy as if we were running an engine unconnected with the drive transmission through which work can be acomplished.

Or consider the living energy of the waves, of the wind, of the waterfall and ask why we are so slow to use it, to harness it to creative achievement? The analogy with the time as currency strikes us here. There is a country saying 'When God made time He made plenty of it'. The potentials unharnessed run to waste. This is all part of the prodigality of Nature – always plenty but only infinitessimal use made of it. Let us include money, in the sense of wealth, in the same category. Unused, unshared, it becomes a burden, a reason for anxiety since loss may threaten. There is a totally fundamental necessity if we are to enjoy a good life, that of *taking*, *holding*, and *giving* again. Let us remember always the deadness and barren surrounding of the Dead Sea, it takes the great life-giving river into its depths and holds it there. But there is no outlet, no flow is possible, no fish swim in its waters and the surrounding shores are infertile.

Unspent energy, unemployed, undemanded by others creates feelings of unwantedness which are very hard to bear. In some families the children have no initiative for either work or play, looking always to others to show them what to do. This may well derive from a lack of encouragement operating between child and adult even in infancy. Encouragement reinforcing spontaneous wishes helps the child to take the next step, not awaiting parental direction, approval or disapproval, using his own libido, his own inborn energy, his own capacity to choose and decide. In this way the child matures, he finds within himself the urge to do things, to make objects, to create something needed and acceptable. The parent who co-operates by valuing and approving the gift stirs up further initiative in the offspring and such attitudes have far reaching effect. When he becomes an adult he finds things to do, not waiting for a job to be put into his hands by others. In such a situation we are aware that the energy is flowing and we can perceive that we need never underestimate what even one individual can initiate and accomplish. There is a contagion about such people; others tending to gather round them are stimulated

into activity and a new creativity in art, craft, music or drama –
endless possibilities – come into being and the community acquires
new life.

Where does this energy-giving initiative and ability in the
individual come from? Is it not our birthright, each of us holding
great capabilites which sadly often fail to develop and flourish
Remember Bergson's words that each newborn child *is* a bundle of
possibilities. Sadly, one by one unused, undemanded, unwanted,
they fall out and disappear.

Seeing energy, then, as currency, we can recognize it is available,
not doubting its source in the Infinite. Throughout a lifetime putting no embargo on its use by reasoning that we are too young or
too old, too stupid or too intelligent, too strong or too weak, let
us constantly speculate about the direction of our lives, thinking
of life as a path, a way, and asking what may lie beyond the next
turning. We must be content to not-know, but can we follow the
advice of ancient Chinese wisdom,: "Keep your eyes on a star and
your feet on the path"?

Unlike money, energy cannot easily be stored. There is an
analogy here with electricity, and, I am tempted to think, with
love. No saving up today because there will be great calls on you
tomorrow, but rather, perhaps, a need to encourage today's flow
so that you will be ready for tomorrow's demand.

Shall we ask at this point how physical and spiritual energy are
related? Can one be equated with the other? Does the energy of the
spirit become a substitute for bodily strength? Old age teaches us
that this indeed may be the case. The tissues of the body waste
with the passing of the years and although much can be done by
maintaining an active physical life, yet the days of feebleness
inevitably arrive. If I may write personally I would say that as we
grow old, wisdom lies in accepting an altered rhythm of life
without either guilt or resentment, recognising that we cannot lay
down any rules for the day's work, but rather take it as it comes,
glad when the energy flows and we can keep going, but willing to
give in to fatigue with the necessity for rest and sleep.

The practice of meditation becomes of increasing importance.
Its value seems to lie in connecting us to the deeper layers of the
unconscious, to a level even deeper than in sleep, from which we
can expect an uprush of psychic strength. In old age many are afflicted with sleeplessness; perhaps they expect longer hours of sleep
than are necessary, and here meditation may well come to the

rescue. It is a simple practice. Be mindful of your breathing: aware, conscious of the incoming, outgoing breath with the rising and falling of your stomach. Thoughts will of course arise and interrupt your concentration. Attend to them, let them go, and again put your attention on the breathing. Energy, like the wind that blows has a source, an origin, but it lies beyond our ken; we are not consciously aware of its whence and whither.

Long before men used steam or electricity as motive power, the wind filled the sails of their boats and turned the wheels that brought water from the wells, and we should remember how very recently our windmills have been abandoned in favour of electric power. Wind, breath, spirit, life itself in essential being, a source not ourselves on which man depends. "Glory to Him whose power (energy) working in us does infinitely more than we can ask or imagine." So let us set our sails to receive and use that energy which awaits our co-operation.

However great or small our sea-faring craft may be, clipper fully rigged or a Kontiki raft, let us seek out and find the Trade Winds. Sailing with them, trusting to the certainty of their strength and direction, we travel safely towards the goal. What if one day they fail and we find ourselves in the doldrums? They too must be part of life's pattern to teach us more about acceptance, expectation, patience and hope.

Anxious, neurotic people come to me as patients with the complaint that their energy is *blocked*. The use of this word block, blockage, suggests water supply in need of a plumber. The work I have been undertaking for so many years often brings to mind the similarities between these two kinds of work: patient investigation as to the location of the trouble, an opening up of the site and then skill in dislodging the offending rubbish. What brings the plumber on the scene is an interference with the supply of water. Instead of an active steady flow there is only a dribble with no force behind it. Psychic flow we call libido, lack of libido means lack of energy, restoration of flow brings great relief. It is marvellous to turn on the tap and get all you need or want. It is equally marvellous to find energy restored when the blockage in the psyche has been dealt with. Incidentally may I say that patients often ask 'Can I do this work? How would I train? How long would it take?' The answer might well be that the training is in the nature of an apprenticeship, and that a plumber's apprenticeship is five years.

To return to the understanding of what leads us to be deprived of energy. The answer, by and large, is that it is anxiety, which is early recognized as a form of fear. In all animal life this seen as an instinctual shrinking from danger; in the animals whose nature resembles the human we find fear, the life-preserving instinct as an element in the emotional life. Necessary and 'good' in itself when it serves us, urging us to keep the safe path, warning us of the risks, dangers, threats in the dark unknown, it can be a good servant to humanity. Things, however, at times go wrong and fear takes over, dominating the personality, now no longer a servant but a master. It attaches itself fortuitously to the circumstances of every-day life, so that we may fear to leave home, fear to cross a street, fear to eat certain foods, fear to meet certain people. There is no end to those irrational derivatives of fear which we call anxiety.

A kindly friend coming to see me recently said "Remember tomorrow is to be a hard and busy day for you. Today take time to rest". My friend seems unaware that energy is current (using the analogy of electricity). We must be aware that, like electricity, energy must flow, it needs to be used. There are great possible resources for the harnessing of physical energy from the mountain torrents, from the waves, from the tides, from the splitting of the atom. But whence comes psychic energy? Its secret lies deep in the unconscious.

When we consider time and money in terms of currency, it is availability that is important. Can we take what we need here and now? Even more, perhaps, is it there for others when they make demands upon us?

Electricity in our houses flows from the plug to the light-bulbs, radiators and other apparatus we acquire and use to bring comfort and luxury into everyday life. Invisibly leading to the plugs are the live wires from the mains. High power wires feed the house mains and beyond them the transformers regulating the strength of the current so that it serves our purposes, supplying light, heat and energy to our appliances. Because of this transformer we are able completely to detach ourselves from the fear that the electricity will be destructive. Hot water comes to us through the tap at the right temperature because a thermostat was installed at the same time as the heater which uses electrical energy, now the source of heat, to raise the temperature of the water to the desired level. I have known anxious people who so distrusted this control system that they were unwilling to install a water heater.

Can this heater be the Hidden Self where, according to St. Paul,

Christ lives in our heart through faith? Jung teaches of the Self as the soul in contact with the Unconscious, nourished by its wholeness, energized by its power, becoming the live wire through which we transmit to others the riches of the limitless love of God. "Glory be to Him", Paul writes, "whose power working in us does infinitely more than we can ask or imagine." Is this not a symbol, an image of what the Creative Spirit has planned for humanity, that we should be the vehicles, the channels, of power other than our mortal own, though which the world is transformed?

Electricity supplies us with light and heat and power. Can we lay hold on life-giving spiritual energy, committing ourselves to its service, to bring the light of consciousness, the warmth of love and the healing gift that make all things new? Hope and seek for the entrance into each of our lives of the promised Spirit of Truth, the Holy Spirit which is waiting to take over from our feeble childish striving.

What are the factors we must acquire which lead us to a commitment to serve our fellow men? How can we 'lay hold on life'? When our Lord chose his twelve disciples, St. John reports Him as saying "You have not chosen me but I have chosen you and ordained you".

Evidence that our life in the body is only part of an immeasurable life-history is gaining ground today. We may even say that the work of Edgar Cayce in America, of Joan Grant and of Dr. Arthur Guirdham in Britain, provide irrefutable evidence, the acceptance of which makes great sense and sheds much needed light on what is happening to us, and to men and women throughout the world today. The reincarnation theories teach us that each of us is an entity, a spirit, which avails itself of a body through which the spirit is always acquiring experience with the possibility of maturity and growth. From previous lives many lessons have been learned but an infinity of wisdom lies open ahead of each of us.

In Jesus we are shown a human being who has grown to his full dimension, fully conscious, fully loving, holy, sinless, accepting fully the Will of God. He has fulfilled the cycles of life and is now received into unity with God, whom He calls the Father. He assures us that He is the first-born of many brethren. Does that mean that in the course of time or outside it other humans are becoming purified so that they too will be absorbed in the Godhead? We are not conscious of this happening around us. Yet something is happening, we know, in the spiritual world and many more than we can guess may be following the Good Shepherd and may be chosen "to live in the house of the Lord for ever", ending their long journey through the ages. Meantime let us hold to it and comfort ourselves and others with the assurance "I am Spirit". I have a body, disposable sure enough, but while it is alive let us use it to serve the Eternal Purpose.

## Money as Currency

What a strange thing money is! Originally they say beads were exchanged for goods that were desired. Later coins came into use, at first bearing some relationship in value to the metal of which they were minted – gold, silver, copper, nickel, bronze and other alloys. Then paper money, the pound notes of no intrinsic value but representing cash and more easy to carry and transport than heavy coin. Cheques, bonds, promissary notes and other pieces of paper came into use, taking the place of coins and notes but with a difference – that they could no longer be easily used as currency. There were crossed cheques, payable only to the one, not changing hands nor being available for any transaction as are coins and notes. Misers were said to keep bags of gold in their cellars and stockings full of cash were often found stored away 'safely' when the owner died.

The banks keep our money safe in one of several possible ways. There is the current account, where money is available instantly on demand, but also the deposit account, where interest accrues, though the money is not so immediately available. Then there are investments. The money is 'locked up' in shares, usually for relatively long periods, and thus is not current. Sometimes I am told of stupid old ladies who keep far too much money in their curent account or of others who forget all about their deposits and investments and never have enough money for their current needs; they believe themselves to be poverty-stricken, whereas there is plenty of money but they have forgotten about it: they have repressed memories of their wealth.

To think of money psychologically creates difficulty for many people who believe it to be entirely tangible, a matter of coins and notes. Yes, of course money is tangible currency. Doesn't it run through your fingers and don't we run out of cash? Unlike energy and time, about which we use the term current, it exists in the material world, is handled and seen. It is so obvious in outer reality in a way that neither time nor energy can be. We cannot fail to be aware of a pile of bank-notes, nor of a bagful of silver coins.

There is a way of living, however, in which money has a non-material, spiritual quality. Its movement obeys laws we cannot understand but on which we can learn to depend. Once embarked on this way of living, knowing that when service is demanded for the good of humanity the money will always come, all we, as instruments of life's purposes, need do is to set foot on the territory awaiting our enterprise and to expect and await results arising from our availability.

True enough, many will laugh at us, throwing doubt on our faith, since they only know money as coin or paper, but they need not deflect us from our purpose. Money will serve us when we no longer allow it to master our lives. As we become increasingly aware of this attitude to life, we shall find much joy in witnessing to what we recognise as the work of the Spirit, which is so infinitely much greater than ourselves. Life becomes all of a piece, full of synchronicities and free from untoward accidents. "The earth is the Lord's and the fulness thereof". Let us take this as affirmation that as earth's creàtures our needs are supplied. Are there conditions? Undoubtedly, yes – but each of us who sees beyond the material into the spiritual realm, each of us who gives up the service of mammon – that is of money – is doing something towards the establishment of ultimate good, call it what we may.

## Cash Flow

I had a visitor today whose work lies largely in the teaching of modern dance. Up to now I had thought of this as difficult because it involved memory of a sequence of movements. But no. it is something different – an awareness of *flow*. "Beginning with awareness of the hands I can allow them to move, to continue movement. I need not remember how I have been taught to move them but rather, by relaxing, loosening anxiety as to whether I am 'doing it right', allow the unconscious to take charge and to direct the course of the movement." Flow, she said, is the important word and we went on to talk about currency. I was fascinated that she shared my views about money, not as bank balance, nor as securities or capital, but as available for present need. She introduced me to the term cash-flow, which seems also to have become current parlance in certain non-commercial circles – circles where it is customary to realise the spiritual rather than the material aspect of daily life.

Another of my younger friends tells me that cash flow is about money never lying idle. It must constantly be in use; no miser's bag or stockings stuffed with notes to be found after you have died. It must not even stay in the bank current account too long; it must change hands, be of use in the community. We must be ready to part with it, to obtain what we need or others need.

Perhaps we can see among our friends three different attitudes to money. Those who like to have money in the bank think of it as security against 'an evil day'. They anticipate times of want and deprivation. In my life-time there has been a change in our thinking about this, particularly amongst the younger people. The State will see to it that we are not deprived in our old age, not even if we lose our health or the work on which our income has depended. The State will take care of us. Still many of us prefer to have a 'nest-egg' rather than an overdraft. They may belong to a group who do not enjoy spending. They have no pleasure in watching the cash flow. The analogy is that water is of more value in the reservoir than in the stream.

Others belonging to a secure category like to spend their money on things. It may be on books and journals, on personal possessions or on new furniture, pictures or other decorations for the home. Women may like to have piles of bed and table linen. There are endless possibilities for satisfying the acquistive instinct and we can notice how, in common with all instinctual drives, it can be a good servant, but when it takes hold and becomes compulsive, a bad master.

To a third category belong those who are always on the outlook for new experiences, going places, seeing people of different cultures and ways of living. Such folk do not grudge the money they spend on going abroad, greatly facilitated nowadays by the availability of air travel. This desire to explore is instinctual. Nomads took to travel long before men had settled homes and fields, and the desire to see far countries is still with us. Marco Polo had no modern equipment. Does something in us still envy him his courage in freeing himself from the security of his own land as he set forth to see what lay beyond the eastern horizons? Today we keep links with home through letters and telecommunication but in those days the severance might well be complete and the return extremely doubtful.

Today's exploring spirit does not confine itself to physical travel but finds satisfaction in reading and imagination with their endless possibilities for investigation of mystery made possible with the invention of apparatus and techniques which are coming into own lives with amazing acceleration.

Cash flow? This third category of the exploring mind needs money but this acquires insignificance when the project is sufficiently magnificent! Dollars were available for man's journey to the moon and the Apollo projects took precedence over our duty to feed our starving fellow men. We must ask ourselves why and perhaps find the answer in the original conflict in man's psyche – 'I want'. 'I want to go to the moon' lies deep in the unconscious in the infantile equipment whereas 'You ought' and even 'I ought to be concerned about the plight of the Third World' is derived from the outer influences. Freud calls them super-ego demands. They are less powerful than those of the Id, the libido which says 'I want' and has its roots in the ultimate being. Shall we call it the Ground of our Being? – and let our minds stray outwards towards the cosmic?

There have always been people in the world who knew that money was intangible and became available when the cause for which it seemed necessary was all-important. All through my life I have been told about Quarrier's Homes in Scotland for destitute unwanted children which were established and still operate without any advertised demand for money. The Chinese Inland Mission had a similar record, the money flowed in to the hands of the founders. To-day the Rudolf Steiner homes which care for children in special need multiply their finance giving no cause for anxiety. Our own work in Edinburgh, the Davidson Clinic for the treatment of people suffering in mind and body was started literally without 'cash' but it operated withouts debts and overdrafts for twenty-five years and today, even more than in its life-time, is recognised as having kept a flame burning, the flame of psychoanalysis, and not just for those who could afford it.

Cash did flow in and out of our banking account, sometimes in gifts of a thousand pounds and more, sometimes in small sums raised by humble efforts. The patients paid according to their ability and the staff gave liberally of their time and talents, since the work was *what they wanted to do* and satisfied them in a way that material wealth never could. In the twenty-five years of the Clinic's existence, outsiders often upbraided me for the small salaries we paid, but the workers, on the contrary, often expressed thanks for the opportunity afforded for doing the work so dear to them and so satisfying. I was in touch with my colleagues through the years and saw no signs of diminished well-being in their circumstances but rather the contrary. Their fidelity to the work was awarded with sufficiency and comfort. I believe it is true that if our primary aim is service and the bringing of enlightenment into the life of our fellows, then anxiety about our own welfare becomes ridiculous. "Seek ye first the Kingdom and all other things will be added" was seen to be true as our work went on unobtrusively and established, as is now acknowledged, a firm foundation for the many psychological activities alive in Edinburgh today. There is no question of claiming credit for our work since through these years all of us working in the realm of the Unconscious learned to be thankful for great success but yet also acceptant of occasional failure. Gratification with the former must of necessity be balanced by guilt and despair over failure. I like to think that we kept the middle way, no personal elation over success nor depression over results that seemed less satifactory. Let us remember always "Glory to Him whose power working in us does infinitely more than we can ask or imagine". The fidelity and availability of our staff members, with disregard for reward or praise, is what today makes us look back on the Clinic with thankfulness.

Writing the word 'availability' brings to mind incidents which frequently occurred when there seemed to be no vacancy in the analysts' lists for new patients, often in somewhat desperate need: somehow the cases would be fitted in to what already was a very full day's programme! We have noted the word currency as equally applicable to money, time, and energy, three facets of currency, but now a fourth comes into mind – people, and we ask ourselves 'Am I available just now when and where I am needed?' Are we, men and women, God's currency?.

Listen to St Paul's magnificent affirmation of his availability and his reason for confidence "I can do all things through Jesus Christ which strengtheneth me" – energy responding to every demand – an energy having its source in the "Not I", the spirit transmitted into our lives from the Infinite, ever seeking its creativity in our lives.

Have you noticed how, strangely, *at a given time*, a few pence in your pocket is more valuable than a £100 note at home? It may be, for instance, that it is essential you keep an appointment. A bus is passing which is exactly what you need. To pay the fare, pence are more valuable than that £100 at home *at the moment*.

I recall an incident of many years past. My father had been on a month's visit to South Africa. Meeting him when he arrived back off the train in Edinburgh, he had to admit that, by lack of foresight, he had only a penny halfpenny in his pocket. My purse contained a few shillings. How thrilled I was that they were available to buy us some food and see us on the next stage of the journey!

Depressed people are in the habit of grumbling over the scarcity of their energy, but is not the quantity but the availability that may matter just at that moment – to give a piece of needed information, to indicate in which direction a stranger should proceed to reach his destination, even a gesture, a hasty pressure of the hand to someone conscious of social inadequacy. What I have written about the availability of a few coins in time of emergency may well lead us on to wonder if God has ever need of 'the little people' those afflicted with a sense of their own inferiority. Are there crises when such people, because they are on the spot in the here-and-now, are of more value than all the most important people occupied with their own business? Are we, representing the copper money, not at that moment of greater value than the high and mighty at a distance who are not available in an emergency? Again quoting St. Paul, see how he reminds us of this: 'Glory be to Him *whose power working in us* does infinitely more than we can ask or imagine'. Who can imagine what a few coppers can do if available just when needed?

Another recollection of childhood: I was living in the country without contact with shops. We were not given pocket-money. If gifts came our way we were encouraged to put the coins into a savings box. Later they might find their way into a Savings Bank account. The idea of cash-flow was foreign to us! Later, living in a town, sixpence a week could buy quite a lot of sweets or even an occasional ice-cream. This, remember, was before the turn of the century, when a halfpenny was not scorned in the sweet-shops. Representing riches to the child at that date, the poor sixpence is of little value today.

Time doesn't exist in the unconscious – past, present and future are all there in our dreams. So it may be that the coppers of our childhood, the silver of middle life and the paper money of old age are only of value when spent. When they change hands, when they bring us sweet things for our liking, or satisfy our daily need, always we find enough. Our coins are few or many, their value is great or little, but our psychic life – the life of the spirit – takes little heed of time and quantity. The spirit rather than common-sense has charge of our lives. Only yesterday, as I talked to Brother Roland in his hut at the Roslin Community, there was a knock at the door and someone put a large loaf of bread on the table. It was Harvest Thanksgiving Sunday and one of the gifts on the altar was the loaf. How strange! Brother Roland's breadbin was empty and he was puzzling how to feed the community at the next meal. It happens like this, increasingly in our day's experience when we realise with ever greater certainty that God provides according to our needs – the actual need of the present moment. Manna! The word means 'What is it?' Our bread for today. Enough.

Values change. Yesterday's currency is obsolete today. But in His presence we are safe from depreciation and loss. The beauty of the lilies, by God's power, is maintained and our energies remain adequate when we are aware of our use in His service, aware that He uses us as His currency.

## The Flow

In everyday language we talk of life as a journey where we travel on a long road, milestones marking the distances. We are aware of what we have left behind us but have to be content to take each stage as it comes – today. The way ahead of us into the future is hidden – we can only guess where it may take us. The road then is a symbol of life as it is lived in consciousness. We can be aware of the footprints of yesterday.

Unconscious life is more like a river than a road, it carries us as we abandon ourselves to its current. No trace here of yesterday. All we know of the river is that it has its source in the heights that we have not explored and that it is making its way to the sea, to the ocean. Our awareness is limited to the here and now of the passing moment and the movement of the water. Sometimes it seems barely to move as it meanders through flat country, but this same river may have had quite different movement in the course of its existence. Sometimes a rushing torrent, maybe a waterfall, at other times swift yet calm – but always the flow.

We can consider human life as conscious happenings and observe it in day to day work and play in our experience of the world, in our relationship with our fellows, with the obvious loves and hates, attractions and repulsions, meetings and partings, so we may envisage them on the road taking us on our journey. Life, however, has another aspect – the unconscious – only glimpsed in waking life but evident in our dreaming, if we can lay hold on the symbolism and content of the dream. The deep unawareness of sleep is disturbed from time to time by a change in the brain function. The electrical impulses, the brain waves, which are essential to life, take on a different frequency and range. Watching the sleeper we can observe that something is alert; there are rapid movements in the closed eyes, muscles may twitch and sounds, probably unintelligible, give warning of the attempt to speak. Although we may remember little or nothing of this dreaming phase, yet observers tell us that everyone dreams and that the dreaming occures usually four times every night as we sleep. It obviously must be an integral part of our experience and have a part to play in life's purpose. Can we then recognize our unconscious sleeping life, with its dream-bearing function, as having meaning, direction and purpose?

Is it not possible to abandon oneself to the river? Divesting ourselves of unnecessary clothing, the persona or mask , and throwing aside unnecessary burdens, how good it is to take the plunge! The energy is in the river, not in ourselves, and we can abandon ourselves to its flow. In the unconscious there is always movement, life is never static but moving. We watch it in the story of evolution and see it daily as babies are conceived and born and grow to adulthood. Man's spirit too, grows, the psyche develops and matures if he lives wisely, in contact with the Spirit other than his own. He will gradually find that self-interest lessens, his care and love for his fellows gains strength and so his life expands, the channel of life becomes a river and the river widens to the sea. Taking from the source, holding it as we practise the Presence, but always aware of the necessity to give, and of the many who are hungry and thirsty for the living bread and the water of life.

A crown-piece lies among trinkets in a drawer on my dressing table. It is convenient to my hand yet it lies there untouched. A crown-piece is no longer currency. This one minted in 1965 has Winston Churchill's head embossed on it instead of the royal effigy. It celebrates a nation's gratitude and acclaims the virutes of the war-time hero. My crown-piece has a story. It was presented to me with some small formality by my colleagues at the Davidson Clinic in recollection of an incident which took place at the clinic's long lunch table in 1964. A wealthy mill-owner (long since dead) had become interested in what we did. We had been able to rescue a member of his family from the distress of a crisis in relationship. The clinic lunch-hour in those days was a good time to entertain visitors; they would meet the staff and come in contact with the spirit of what was happening between us and our patients. My colleague, who shared the direction of our work with me was well separated at the other end of the long table while our guest sat beside me opposite. My colleague had a naughty streak in him and was murmuring to his neighbour "Do you know what Winifed is up to? She is getting money out of that old boy. I bet you that at this moment she is relating to him how she started the clinic in 1939 with only five shillings." The old boy departed leaving a cheque for £1,000 on the table but when my colleague recounted the story I had to correct him. I asked him "How do you think anyone could engage on such an enterprise on five shillings?" The point is that we started this without any money at all. Later the staff gave me the crown-piece, worth five shillings in those days, saying "Now you have it, what more are you going to do with it?" The coin lies deep in my trinket box, but is symbolic in many ways.

Where is that five shilling piece? Long gone out of currency but still of value – shall I see what it will bring if I take it to the market place today? Better keep it, more worth in its symbolic value than in the few coins that might come in exchange. Since the clinic had its beginning without a bank account, we must inquire on what was it then built? On an idea? My mind travels back to the old dining-table where we gathered for our meals as children. Breakfast, dinner, tea and supper four times daily over many years, much more must have happened than the feeding of our bodies. Knowledge aquired through the asking and answering of questions, even though some questions embarrassed the parents and they evaded answering.

Our paternal grandfather was included in the family for the first ten years of my life – if his presence at meals led to some restriction there were also things to remember. I remember grumbling one day about the weather "Why wasn't the sun shining?" and the response from my father "If the sun weren't shining – none of us would be here – sup up your porridge!" I think an interesting conversation developed on these occasions and in all probablility we were as a rule encouraged to talk. Visitors in plenty came to meals, both simple and learned people, introducing us to other levels of society than our own middle class where we were so complacent.

An incident bearing on the idea leading to the establishment of the Davidson Clinic still seems vivid. A guest, a member of Parliament sharing a meal suddenly out of the blue it seemed, asked my mother what she thought was the most important, or he might have said the most beautiful, text in the Bible. While she was thinking about it, he told us "God hath not given us the spirit of fear but of power and of love of a sound mind". I was a teenager at the time and in my sixth decade when I started the clinic.

The Davidson Church, a congregation in the north of Edinburgh had offered us premises where we could make a beginning to clinic work. This meant I was told, bringing the congregation into sympathy with the project and I was urged to address them from the pulpit at a Sunday morning service. Diffident about this ordeal I suddenly found courage and said "Yes I have the text. 'God hath not given us the spirit of fear, but of power and of love and of the sound mind," – My task was to make clear what the work of psychoanalysis was all about, but to give it in religious language.

"The spirit of fear" I explained was anxiety. Fear is one of the basic instincts with which not only mankind but also the animals are endowed. It has to do with the avoidance of danger, and also with the preservation of life – like all the instincts it is neither good nor bad in itself but a part of our individual inheritance. When we are able to use it wisely to serve us, fear (like fire) is a good servant. The spirit of fear is anxiety ('nerves' they called it in those days) and when anxiety masters us we are in danger of becoming aliens in society. "Not fear but power" which we call energy. It is our birthright, but how magically we can lose it when fear and anxiety block its flow. Not fear but love – the good relationship which develops when trust in God and trust in our fellow men replaces our anxiety. "Not fear but a sound mind" the result of which is tranquility.

Pathetically, the physicians of the psyche – we call them psychiatrists – are still unaware of the need to help the anxious, neurotic, worried, indolent, disturbed patients to find their way into becoming again endowed with energy, love and tranquillity. So that day in 1939 I gave this message from the Davidson Church pulpit. One of the audience was Sir John Falconer, at that time Edinburgh City Treasurer, but later Lord Provost. I remember so well his smiling face as he responded to the message – it reminded him he said of sermon they used to hear in the Highlands when he was a boy. From that day, he helped us with his support and because of his certainty that the message was true, he remained chairman of our Board until he died. I like to remember how he used to tell me that his own life was greatly strengthened by the awareness that God's will for his people is *not fear but love*.

Currency and that crown-piece where are you? Are you lost in this long story of the clinic? Before he died, my husband, Frank Rushforth asked me always to remember to remind the staff of the clinic that it was *not an institution but a movement*. How true this can be seen clearly in retrospect.

## Availability

Writing about currency (flow, libido) of money, time and energy, I began to think how we, as human beings, are also part of the flow in the great river of life. Abandoning ourselves to the current we float peacefully, or, if we are inclined to swim, there is great pleasure in merging our energy with the flow of the stream. There is the co-operation between personal and impersonal, the two energies merging to carry us, without effort, out into the wider spaces.

So with us all, as men and women, are we able to throw ourselves without fear into life as it flows? Do we go with it, full of pleasure and realisation of effortless movement? Sad, afflicted people among us seem unable to see which way the river flows, and struggle against it. They complain bitterly about their exhaustion and fatigue, about their advancing years, their ill-health, and expectation of trouble. Against the stream, their energy, unrewarded by achievement, meets frustration and disappointment, obvious in their looks, gestures, attitudes and attainments. Discouragement spreads from such individuals to those with whom they come in contact, till we find areas of pessimism, negative, anxious people infecting their neighbours with the fear that life is not worth living. When we commit ourselves to the positive, to the awareness that life has purpose and meaning, that there is energy with which we must get in contact, then we can make the best of each day as it comes. If we are willing to let life live in us, accepting what it brings, as the days pass, without resentment, without demanding that circumstances should change to accommodate our wishes, but rather using all that happens to carry us further on the way to fulfillment, then truly we have found wisdom.

People who have this attitude are full of contagious influence upon others, giving encouragement so that they too will take advantage of the positive, outgoing spirit linking with Nature's creativity, bringing new life as it passes. Here, again, is the flow, the current of feeling – 'vibrations' people call them nowadays – transmitted at a deeper level of the psyche than conscious thought. Here, contact with others does not depend on words, but on finding the 'wavelength' in others through which communication takes place.

We defined currency of money as that which is available in one's pocket or purse, to hand when needed. Are some people like this? We may think them open, willing, watching for opportunity to help and to give. What do they give? We talk of lending an ear. Indeed, the faculty of listening is greatly to be prized since, through listening, we establish relationship from which much may happen to both parties. Through sharing, fertilisation of feeling and thinking occurs, tentative ideas being either established as truth, or rejected when they do not ring true. Listening brings understanding through which what was unconscious comes into consciousness and a further flow is established, comparable to the streaming of light into darkness – this too is symbolic of understanding. To avail ourselves of opportunity is to keep moving. The word is derived from the Latin *porta*, a door, so let us think of movement, doors opening, new vistas, new calls upon us to look and see, to listen and understand.

The young child begins life with a need to be the centre of care and attention but, as he gains maturity, a change takes place, and the need to serve takes precedence over the desire to be served. Gradually, the truth dawns, that to give does not impoverish but rather enriches, and we realise the law of love, that the more we give, the more we get, and lose our fear of parting with our resources, knowing that unconscious, intangible forces are at work, through which we are becoming one with the others in the stream of life. Our ability grows and strengthens to see the needs of others, and find a willingness to serve them, without a sense of deprivation in the giving. .

Currency again, but no longer of money, energy and time. We find ourselves inter-current, inter-dependent, ready to serve and give, able to touch, to hold in the passing, able also to let go, respecting the freedom of the others as well as their need. We recognise that their independence is, at times, so important to them, when loosening the bonds that unite parent and child, teacher and pupil, even doctor and patient. When adulthood, wisdom and health are established there is always renewed a taking, holding and giving again, and life has greater meaning and purpose. Our small circles enlarge, and the radiance from the Centre finds an ever-widening field.

Channels, conduits, pipelines – applying the concept behind these words to ourselves or others, we postulate a source, an Infinite Resource, which will not fail since it is linked to energy beyond humanity, cosmic, 'eternal in the heavens'. It is there for us, but our life-task is to avail ourselves of this power awaiting the demand that it should be used. Are we as individuals, then, reponsible? Is it in our own choice to lay ourselves open to the flow? When we are thinking of involving some of our friends, and fellow workers, we are sure to find some who are too busy, who have no time, who are perhaps rather indignant that we should assume their possible co-operation – can't we realise how fully-booked their time and energy is? So much may fail at that point and a whole possiblity come to naught. Others? Can we find those who will always make time, create a space in the day to lend an ear, to lend a hand, through which our project gains energy and something more happens? It may well be that a forward step in evolution is achieved. Willingness is all, and we may well link this with our petition, 'Thy will be done'. Can we make our response no longer just the 'I want' of the child, but now 'I am willing' to follow in the steps of the Divine Shepherd to whom we pray, 'Lead us', 'Deliver us'?

Only in recent years has the practice of meditation become widespread and acceptable increasingly, both in this country and further abroad. It is, undoubtedly, a way of laying ourselves open, open to 'That' which we hesitate to give a name, and which, as St. Paul reminds us, "working through us does infinitely more than we can ask or imagine."

Mankind, then, shares in currency, along with time, money and energy, when we become conscious of the great flow of Divine Love and Purpose which is there for us. Going with the stream, all things are possible, and when we act as conduit, channel, pipeline, then we serve the Divine Will. Availability is all.

# Personal Themes

## What Would Have Happened?

"What would have happened to me if I had never met you Dr. Rushforth?" Maisie, who asked this unanswerable question, is one of many women who have come to me in their mid-twenties unhappy because of the realisation that life is not satisfying them. Other girls with whom they were at school or college have married and are bringing up children. Why do men pass them by? Why, although they acquire boy friends, does the relationship not mature? What is 'it' that makes people fall madly in love? Why are the boys or men attracted so unsuitable, either tied to their mothers with no mind of their own, or old enough to be her father, looking for a wife with whom they can now settle down after unsatifying bachelor days? Even more frequently they are married men.

Maisie's question linked up with Peggy's distraught anger which I had been encountering in recent weeks. "Why," she asked, "could no one have told me what was wrong with me and helped me to find myself? I tried so hard. Could my minister help? He seemed quite at sea; his quotations from Scripture made no sense, nor did his willingness to pray for me. I tried a psychiatrist, reaching him only after many futile interviews with the family doctor. He listened, it is true, for the best part of an hour, told me that I must not be anxious, advised me to keep in touch with my own doctor who would prescribe pills for my nerves when they became too jittery, but made no arrangement for further interviews."

Peggy then heard of a counselling service in connection with a modern congregation. To get in contact with this service in a neighbouring town involved expense in time and money that she could ill afford. Peggy's voice rose to a scream of frustration and fury as she described the interview. It shed no light at all on the condition for which she needed help, and ended with "the old fool" patting her kindly on the back and saying, "One of these days you will find yourself with a kind husband and a nice family of dear children and will be able to forget all this unhappiness".

I expected the neighbours to come to Peggy's rescue as she screamed for help retrospectively. Now, we both realised, even her wish to bear children was gone. She had already divorced one immature and impotent husband and, her present man, although a distinguished philosopher, lived so completely in the world of unreality that she had given up hope of their being able to make a family an economic possibility.

Peggy, however, had guts. Her spell of psychotherapy with me had involved air-travel from overseas and expense that emptied the reserves in her bank. The letter that I had from her after her return reported that, although outer circumstances in their marriage were difficult, her husband had 'improved' during her absence and that she found herself able to be angry with him eliciting a surprising response from his philosophic self-absorption. Peggy's rage against society for not providing adequate help when she was in her later teens and early twenties is often expressed in my consulting room. "Why didn't I know you when I was sixteen?" I remember this question asked by a woman in her late forties, married to a long-suffering husband, with no family to satisfy and comfort them and little prospect of the years ahead being either creative or anything but boring.

Another of the same age, Janet – women tend to seek help from analysis as they approach the menopause – was equally vociferous in her complaints. These focused, as is usual, on the mother's lack of identification with her as daughter. A mother who does not value her own womanhood is discontented to bear female children, is known to remark to neighbours and visitors on her disappointment that her first-born was not a son, and to show obvious pride and elation over the contents of the pram – the newly-arrived man-child.

Ex-babies have a hard time in any family, but Janet's mother, herself one of seven sisters, was unduly exultant over the boy's birth. Janet was gifted musically in contrast to her mother. Instead of rejoicing in this as supplementing the family's value, the mother was jealous of the little daughter and attached no value to her achievements, either in the prizes she collected in musical festivals and such-like occasions, or in the pleasure other people expressed on hearing her make music. Janet had, when she came to me, completely denied her musical gifts, never touched the piano, had forgotten her songs. I shared her delight when she found herself suddenly *wanting* to share in her sons' music, playing duets with them, and joining in their singing. Like Peggy she had married an inadequate husband, a man seeking for the good mother denied him in his infancy.

An interesting and not uncommon situation in this family was that although both Janet and her husband were living so far below their potential, he as a semi-invalid, she as his bitterly resentful house-keeper and companion, yet the sons were extremely gifted. Janet despised her husband and had a violent hatred of his aristocratic family, her in-laws. He had little appreciation of the intellectual middle-class family with whom he had almost accidently allied himself, but mother Nature had taken a hand in the marriage. The boys had a genetic inheritance undeveloped but transmitted through both parents.

I like to think that the further development of their lives became possible when their mother had worked out her early furious resentments against her own parents in analysis. During this process she became able to assess her in-laws more objectively, and to find value in the ancestry which she was now instrumental in tranmitting to her sons. In her husband's library she found evidence that his forebears had been men of great distinction who had served their generation faithfully. She could now be proud that, whatever his personal inferiority, she had been allotted the privilege of fostering the inheritance.

Janet reported, as analysis went on, the "improvement" in her husband, just as Peggy had done. In both cases, and in many others, as the conflicts in the life of the analysand are dealt with, the family tension becomes less acute and, as in Janet's case, a happy family situation is established. The children are then in an atmosphere of peace and relaxation in which they are not distracted from the course of their own emotional development.

Am I a prideful analyst? Well, Stephen who worked so hard at his resentments, and in consequence was able to live in peace within walking distance of his home, reported that Dr. R. was pretty clever, she had analysed a patient whom she had never met who lived four hundred miles from her base in Edinburgh – namely, his mother!

I began to write about Maisie and shall finish this chapter by recording several facts that she passed on to me, when we had our last analytical hour. First I may observe that she was not a long-term case coming twice weekly over the years. She came when she could, from another town, at infrequent intervals. The points in her favour were her youth, now 27 (I first saw her four years ago); her intelligence, she was an honours student at the University; and the fact that she was a 'seeker', dissatisfied with that level of life on which one is constantly frustrated and subject to accidental disasters.

So now this is what she was able to tell me a day or two ago about her recent life. She had been on a cruise and had been able to relate herself to people of her own age, feeling accepted yet not too deeply involved. The men she met were all married. Two of them, travelling on business without their wives, had been friendly and even affectionate but she was not tempted into emotional entanglements and both they and she had enjoyed the experience. Maisie then reported a series of fruitful conversations, between her mother and herself. She was temporarily living in her parents' house and could not but be aware of the widening gap between them. She had had an opportunity of conversations with her mother begun by a bitter tirade of the mother against her husband. During the analysis Maisie had frequently discussed the situation. At one time she had threatened to take her mother's place and relate herself to the man of the family, cajoling him into being more sociable, and drawing him into her own interests and occupations.

Fortunately this had been unsuccessful and now I was listening to what she had been able to do with his wife, her mother. This lady was still young and attractive. She had a job in an office and was on extremely good terms with her boss, whose wife and four children were friendly to her. They had come to be the focus of her interest instead of her husband and household.

So now Maisie, seeing the situation clearly since her own part in it had been observed, was able to talk it over, listening patiently to the mother's point of view, not denying her right to be bitter, but gradually enabling her to see that she was giving to another man and his family the interest, care and attention so badly needed at home. This stream of loving interest could only act as poison in the boss's life, whereas, if directed where it belonged, to her own man and his needs, it could be healing and do something to restore the relationship threatened by disruption. Now optimistic and ready to leave home in the near future, Maisie could smile and say, "Things are much better already".

Her third achievement was with a woman friend whose marriage was in difficulties. This woman had one son and, having decided that the father's influence on him was intolerable, had taken an all-or-nothing step of sending him away to live with her relatives and attend school in a distant village. She had decided not to visit him but to allow him to return for school holidays.

At the end of a year he had reacted by becoming delinquent, had stolen money and become an accomplished liar. From her own experience Maisie knew what parental separation could do to a child and begged her friend to make arrangements to visit him regularly and keep in good relationship with him. Instead of condemning him for his bad behaviour she was to see it as his reaction to her rejection of him. Maisie could now report not only a happier mother-son relationship but also insight gained in the school where the boy's master had been drawn into the situation and was now co-operative and not judgemental.

Maisie has qualities of intuitive understanding and of generous loving-kindness inherent in her personality. Through her analysis these have been liberated. She is now a smiling, happy woman able to avail herself of opportunity. Through her, others gain insight, are more able to understand and therefore to forgive, so that her life adds to the sum of human happiness and brings The Kingdom a step or two nearer in the harsh world of today's suffering.

*(1967)*

# Ambivalence

A 'casual' patient was the next to be seen that day, not an analysand whom I could expect to meet twice weekly for the next few weeks or months. This patient rings up occasionally when he is in deep waters, a middle-aged lawyer who had attained an eminent position in his profession in spite of much emotional insecurity and ill-health. Mounting anxiety had goaded him into phoning, and, contrary to his usual practice, he had told his wife that he thought he would be the better for a few talks with me. I gathered she had been thankful, so I guessed the tension between them had been considerable. It all began, he said, when his wife had slipped on the stairs of their house and had been found unconscious, having knocked her head as she fell. He had been panic-stricken but had summoned help and accompanied her in the ambulance to hospital where she spent a few days during which he felt terribly upset. This was some months ago; she was now, as usual, well and busy. Why, he asked, should his anxiety be so persistent?

It did not, as a matter of fact, begin with this incident. As he talked to me reminiscently he remembered that when he was a small boy, perhaps six years old, his mother had had some similar accident. It had occurred in the street; she had fallen and lay there motionless, and, to his mind, dead. He was, naturally enough, panic-stricken and very much afraid of the policemen who came to the rescue and took them both in an ambulance to hospital. He seemed to re-live this incident with distress and remarked how curious it was that it had been forgotten. He had not thought of it for years.

In another way, too, "it all began" when first he found that the lovely gay interesting bride, a divorcee whom he had married not too early in his life, had other qualities as well as her beauty and her wit. She was extremely jealous of his other relationships, particularly with women. (I, too, am a woman!) She had from the first adopted a maternal attitude to him so that he felt at times that his position was more that of an eldest son than of her equal. It had to be admitted that she bossed the whole family, made the decisions, often landed him in embarrassing situations, and in fact that he now often resentfully felt "I wish she were dead". This caused him great distress as he admitted it. Perhaps he thought he was the only husband to harbour such thoughts! "I know," he said, "I *ought not* to feel like this." Anxiously he looked at my face to see how solemnly I must be condemning him. Instead, I am afraid, he found me laughing. I confessed that throughout my life I had always disposed of troublesome relations by murdering them, or at least by wishing they were dead. This did not really surprise him, and he began, quite usefully, to justify himself and to tell me how really tiresome his wife could be. She was *not* a good housewife, nor even a good cook; she tended to be late even for important functions. She continually lost important papers and at times became bad-tempered and made life hell. I was very sympathetic and joined him in the idea that her death would solve many of his troubles.

This, however, set him off in the opposite direction. How beautiful she still can be when dressed for a party! How good she is at remembering who people are and standing by when he is at a loss. How her wit still attracts to her the more lively members of their set. How she really is kind hearted and makes him wish he had more sympathy for people in trouble. Then he assures me that *never never* is he sorry that he married her and that I can have no idea at all of how wonderful their life together has been. He is puzzled and deeply distressed by his ambivalence and again extremely guilty that he ever had any bad feelings against her.

Gradually as we talk, he realises that he is not alone in his problem, that it is indeed common in all relationships. Even, he now thinks, he may have been ambivalent towards his very dear, precious mother. Was it possible, I wonder, that he heaved big sighs of relief when he realised she was dead? I didn't ask him this question. It is at times too shocking to realise our human situation in its crudity. The grief over her death, which he still remembers, is more acceptable to our idea of the perfect mother-son relationship. This article on Ambivalence, "Heads and Tails of the Penny", seems particularly relevant to my work both with 'casual' and more regular patients; it is something to which we can all profitably pay attention in our lives.

(*c.1967*)

# Memorandum
# on Corporal Punishment

The Davidson Clinics in Edinburgh and Glasgow are working in the field of treatment of neurotic illness. As a staff we are engaged in the analysis of sick persons some of them labelled psychopathic or delinquents, others with the more respectable labels of psychosomatic patients or psycho-neurotics, depressives, etc.

In order to do this work adequately it is necessary for the staff to be analysed individually, that is to discover the motivation of their own conduct. When this is understood it becomes impossible to blame, chastise or castigate the patients, however untoward or socially unacceptable their behaviour may be.

"There but for the grace of God go I" must not only be a facile word on our lips but it must be an expression of awareness of the self-centredness and of the law-breaking aspect of our own lives. Only so, by a measure of indentification with the wrong-doer, can we hope to redeem him as a member of society. Surely these unfortunate people are what they are, and act as they do, not because they are bad in contrast to our supposed goodness, but because through lack of charity, by a sort of moral 'apartheid', we have driven them into the world of the outsider or enemy of society.

Beating is an aggressive act, cruelty inflicted under a mask of righteousness. Its effect on the wrong-doer must inevitably be to make him more resentful, more an enemy of authority than before. Freudian teaching has shown clearly that beating has an effect on the development of normal sexuality. Whenever sexual feeling (genital excitement) is stimulated by flagellation then cruelty instead of love becomes the operative factor in the union of men and women. A vicious circle is started since the father (or his substitute, judge, magistrate or schoolmaster) beats the next generation and so on until "the grace of God" intervenes to break in upon the unholy business. Clinics such as ours do seek to mediate this grace through the technique of analysis, but although our methods are adequate our resources for the wide-spread distress throughout the country are sadly inadequate.

Teaching of the public has its place and many people can perhaps be encouraged to think again about this matter when knowledge of the unconscious processes is available. How disturbing it is to find those in the highest places still apparently unaware of the significance of their desire to inflict punishment of this nature. Perhaps the day will come when we can ask that our judges and magistrates at least should submit to some measure of analysis before they are 'elevated' to the Bench, – lest they should, by their desire to punish, set again in motion these influences which make for enmity between individuals, communities and nations.

*From Dr. W. Rushforth, Hon. Medical Director of The Davidson Clinic, Edinburgh.1960*

*Editors' Note:* This Memorandum was sent to the Advisory Council on the Treatment of Offenders, in response to a letter from its chairman, Sir Patrick Barry, published in *The Sunday Times*. It was reprinted in the *Davidson Clinic Bulletin* (July 1960). There is no record of any reply to her letter!

"God has no other hands but ours . . . . . . . ."

St Theresa

# What Do I Want To Do?

This is Monday morning, nearly a week since I began to write in earnest. I am late today – 9.30 instead of 9 o'clock which is my target. It *seemed* necessary to do some tidying and to water my house plants, picking off withered leaves and blossoms, which awakens in me a question I so often ask my patients, "Is it really necessary?" There are in life certain well-beaten paths, sometimes we call them duty, but they are also convention, if we find ourselves unable to get off them we may think of ourselves as obsessional.

This morning I realise that at the age of 82 I have entered a new phase in my life in which quite a good poster on the road asks simply, "Does it matter all that?" The road is there, and there is only one direction in which I can travel. Perhaps I must learn day by day that it doesn't really matter whether time is as fully occupied as lately I have thought necessary. Yesterday was Sunday and the afternoon and evening had been planned, but till noon a spacious hour or two had been dedicated in my mind to putting my bedroom in order. Many things *ought* to be thrown out, cupboards *ought* to be tidied, dusting certainly was needed and a vacuum cleaner brought into action. Nothing of this was accomplished. It was a sunny morning and I went into the garden to see what flowers I could cut to fill my vases. Nasturtiums are at their best this month. I like to call them "bottled sunshine" and to arrange them with their trailing stems in dark corners where they catch the eye.

Once outside the house it is difficult to go back out of the sunshine – I shall open the garage and put the car ready to start off at 12 noon as arranged. As I run it out – "Oh dear, the windscreen *is* dirty." Cleaning it, I find much more than the windscreen needs to be dealt with and as I fill a bucket and wring out a cloth up come three twelve-year-olds, "Clean your car, ma'am?", and I am at their mercy. Not only the car but also the garage floor, and the garden paths could provide an hour's work for us all.

I have what I call my potting-shed on a wall by the courtyard where the car cleaning was going on. The children became interested in the little pots of cuttings and we shared an interest in how they were growing. Three 'Wandering Sailors' were allocated, but in the end only one child was sufficiently interested to take his plant away with him. "Could we have a hurl, ma'am?" I saw this as a good means of getting them off the premises so we made a big effort to leave things moderately tidy and to return objects where they belonged, and then they packed themselves into the car and off we went round the block for their 'hurl', the Scots word for a 'ride'. The children's faces kept with me all the day and although my allotted task of tidying had not been accomplished, I know that this freedom, this straying on a bypath off the 'ought' road is right for me now.

What do you *want* to do? This question needs to be honoured all through our lives. It cannot be the only guide but unless we ask it of ourselves and others we miss the fun. 'I want' is the word of the instinctual life, of the libido, the psychic energy demanding fulfilment. 'You ought' becomes 'I ought', necessary controlling influence, but frustrating if allowed to be the only criterion of how we live. The art of living must, I think, consist in finding the right balance between I *want* and I *ought* in our lives. Tension is inevitable between them, but tension is creative. If either is allowed to dominate us some sort of destruction is inevitable. Libido unchecked, ultra-permissiveness in parents, the only guide one's own wishes, then we lose sight of the highway and the byways lead to dead-ends and frustration. The opposite pole, too stringent calls of duty, too great a demand that we never deviate from the conventions of family and community, that we discover what is right and stick to it through thick and thin. This way also leads to frustration through which our natural instinctual life suffers distortion and weakens through the attrition of over-control.

In Hamlet's words, "There is nothing either good or bad, but thinking makes it so", the kind of thinking that is judgement condemns or condones. I find in listening to my patients that many of them, like myself, were brought up by mothers who were quite sure that 'there is a right way and a wrong way of doing everything'. Probably I was in my adolescence before I was brave enough to ask my mother, "Is your way *always* the only right way?" I remember a certain hesitation, but it was not prolonged, before the answer came, "Yes, of course". That must have finished a stage in my relationship with her, since it made no sense to me, and from that day I was more free within myself and less certain that mother's way is the right way or at least the *only* right way. *Less* certain, I say, but maternal opinions and ideas are not easily expelled from our patterns of thought and behaviour. My parents had – as all of us have – idealised images of themselves to which they conformed when possible, but such images have feet of clay, and their destruction brings much puzzlement to their offspring and a great sense of guilt to themselves. A completely comical example of this in my father's case perhaps also occurred when I was entering my teens, but my brothers were older and more able to criticise and even jeer. 'The Sabbath day' was observed as utterly different from week-days. Toys and picture books, later on all light literature, were put away – we attended Church and Sunday School – we were given Bible lessons and learned to repeat the metrical psalms. Dinner was a cold meal prepared on Saturday except that the potato pot was set to the side of the hearth and the potatoes cooked themselves while we attended the Morning Service. This enabled the maids as well as the family to go to Church. On Sunday afternoons, in fine weather, Father took us for a walk – perhaps these were infrequent as I do not remember much about them – otherwise we amused ourselves in the garden or stackyard, but there would be no 'rounders' or football with the "cottage children" such as we might play on weekday evenings. Now for the terrible disclosure! One fine Sunday afternoon, a warm sunny day, we *discovered* Father not where he often sat in front of the house but behind the garden hedge, smoking a cigar (he was a non-smoker) and reading *The Strand Magazine*. What could have been more shocking! Later in her life, Mother would knit on Sundays and I believe in the 1914-18 war she, along with other women, knitted during the sermon in Church. Undoubtedly the old order was changing and one of the amusing things about being as old as I am now is to see how utterly different our age is and how the oughts and ought-nots of life have lost much of their power. The Church bells only evoke a very minor degree of guilt when I am sure that I *don't want* to go to church, and the books that I read on Sunday are no different from the week-day literature. If my grandchildren are coming to dinner it is fun to spend the morning cooking, or if someone suggests a picnic on a fine day that is splendid, although I (would) still avoid packing the car while my neighbours pass my door on the way to church!     *(1967)*

# Explosions

In Edinburgh we have a hill – almost a mountain, called Arthur's Seat. In our schooldays, we were taught that it was an extinct volcano and, indeed, I have often picked up pieces of lava on the hillside. I can remember expecting it to erupt again one day, not particularly dreading it, but rather imagining it as of great possible interest and excitement. A patient, living near Ben Lomond, has told me that he had similar feelings that affected him at bedtime. The bedtime prayer of a little boy is often quoted by psychotherapists, "And please God, don't let the boiler burst". A very interesting woman patient of mine, who earned her living as an office cleaner, related to me how, although an immersion heater had been installed in her hot water tank, she would not consider the idea of switching it on. Enquiring why, I got the answer, "In case the boiler bursts". "No", I explained, "when the engineer installed the heater, he also fixed the thermostat", and I tried to make clear to her how this worked. She was, however, quite sure that she would not commit herself to its use. Do we, I wonder, deprive ourselves of the use of much psychic energy because of the fear that it may overwhelm us?

The psychological jargon we use to elucidate these fears is 'all fear is endopsychic', that is, we explain the conscious anxiety by the idea that it symbolises our dread of losing control of our libidinous drives – are we at their mercy, so that any day they might become uncontrollable?

Let us look at a few examples of the direction in which this energy may be deployed in our lives. Early in life, I learned from a school reading-book that fear is a good servant but a bad master. Later, I learned that fear is a part of human endowment and even the newborn infant attaches fear to loss of support – 'Will the maternal arms hold safely'. Early, too, we are taught that loud noises awaken the infant's fear. In so far as it serves the purpose, which develops as the child grows and becomes conscious, fear warns us against danger. We know it as a life-preserving force. If, however, fear gets out of hand, becoming master instead of servant, then man's state can be a sorry one, fear blocking the roads on which his travels should take him to develop his own inner potential and his capacity to communicate, that he may become one with the others in the stream of life.

Fear is a part of our creaturely nature, that is to say, we share it with the other animals, even in some elemental way, it may be, with all living things. What else do we share with our not-yet-human relatives? Very obviously, the hungers and thirsts that sustain our bodies. Serving us well, they give us the physique we need but, when they master us, becoming compulsive, they produce the glutton and the alcoholic. Sexuality, linked to all creativity, has an importance, even above hunger without which individuals deny themselves physical life. Without sex, the race dies, and to create progeny so that humanity holds its place in the world is obviously all-important. Humanity is made, strangely more than animal we are told, in the image of God, so that in mankind the spirit and the body are interconnected. One cannot live without the other, but there is mutual dependence and a great area of common life.

The reproductive functions operate in women for a limited time – roughly thirty-five years, but in males for a longer time. Even in childhood, there is a great differentiation between the sexes, and early attraction and antipathy between male and female. At puberty, childhood gives place to adolescence, with maturation of the testes in the male, the ovaries in the female. The cells necessary for reproduction are now available, spermatazoa in the male, ova in the female as, incidentally, all the bodies assume new proportions, with rapid growth of the limbs and muscular strength developing in the boy, while the body of the girl assumes a roundness and a softness that make her a woman.

Another route for the libidinous energy is anger, an element in human nature which makes itself obvious in the earliest days of life – the angry child screaming because he is bereft of the breast, red in the face, furious at his deprivation. Conventional parents and civilised society tend to disapprove of anger but, without it, we become door-mats, downtrodden, lacking the vitality, the whip-cord which is our birthright. Anger need not be violent and destructive as it is when it becomes master and compulsive, and the bad-tempered, vindictive personality develops. It serves us well when we are conscious of the heat it generates, yet are in control. There is such a possibility as gentle anger – not exploding but rather welling up in the relationship, linked with wisdom and understanding. Here again, we get the energy as a servant used to promote good relationship, not punishing and so giving rise to further hostility and resentment.

Aggression, like anger, may get a bad name, yet our lives are poorer without it. The primary meaning is that of relationship, from the Latin *ad* – towards, and *gradus* – a step, so that the approach to our neighbour depends on the capacity for aggression. Unfortunately, in our society, there is great value attached to goodness in children by which is meant docility, obedience, renunciation of self-will. Until the beginning of the Second World War, with its call-up of all available personnel for the forces, the 'good Scots nannie who stood no nonsense' was still to be found in many families. She extorted obedience and the afore-mentioned evidence of goodness from her wards, and their parents frequently boasted of her success in the achievement of the children's model behaviour. We can now see that there was a great probability of loss in the personality of these children – and it takes great wisdom on the part of parent or nanny to hold the balance between the will of the child and the discipline required by society. It is definitely no fool's job being a parent who repects both of these powerful forces operating in each individual, perhaps at their maximum strength in the early years, 'I want' can fight a fierce battle with 'You ought', before the latter becomes 'I ought'. There seems to be danger in this happening too early in life – hence a maxim for parents 'Don't make them too good too soon'.

A dream, provided recently be a man in a dream analysis group, gives a useful demonstration. "We seemed to visit a very attractive house but, opening a door, found ourselves in the basement. At first, all seemed in good order but, as I wandered round, I found myself in a dark corner with a terrifying animal which was imprisoned behind iron bars. I feared it would break out, and fled upstairs to safety." The basement in dreams can signify the personal unconscious, the area of forgotten memories. In the group, memories of his childhood had begun to stir and, here in his unconscious, he finds a very ugly threatening creature. It had been confined behind prison bars by the disciplining forces of his early years but, now, re-entering the past through analysis, he discovers this aspect of his own psyche "in a dark corner behind iron bars" but in danger of breaking out. Later, we believe, he will face this imprisoned aspect, come to terms with it, allow it to become his ally and give him the strength now locked up and unavailable. This dreamer is young and has the advantage of sharing his dreams with the group, so that he is able to explore the unconscious, the forgotten memories of his childhood. There is great potential in the fearful creature which is now in the process of becoming conscious and no longer dangerous.

In contrast to the threat of destruction, as demonstrated in this man's dream while under analysis, let us look at what happens so often in later life. Let us take as an example a member of the so-called upper class, who has had the (doubtful) benefit of nursery training in his childhood. Obedience, politeness, decorous behaviour are deeply valued, whereas tantrums and any display of anger are frowned upon, and may even be punished by 'smacked bottom', or other nursery disciplines. Let us see him now in his late fifties, a high-ranking army officer or 'boss' at the head of an important institution. Matters do not inevitably go smoothly with his charges but it is difficult for them to understand why he cannot deal with the misunderstandings reasonably. Why the need to lose his temper – a condition not too unlike the tantrums of infancy? The angry man is likely to rationalise his furious feelings by the idea that his subordinates are fools. He is unlikely to recognise that as he ages his defences are weakening, and that his anger is no longer under control but it is getting the upper hand. In his well-disciplined years, it has been locked up behind iron bars in his unconscious – the basement of the aforesaid dream – without the possibility of creative use. Now it is destructive, engendering fear and dislike between him and his subordinates. Instead of his psychic energy – his libidinous strength – flowing in his life, available for good relationship and creative purpose, it is volcanic and destructive.

It is necessary to understand anger as part of life's equipment, without which we are the poorer. The angry years occur early, between the ages of three and four. At this time, there is a great need for holding: physically held tight in his parent's arms the child's anger dies. A further holding is that of understanding, which brings a happy response. Punishment for this childish anger may seem to have value in good behaviour, but the cost of imprisoning the potential is great; the vital energy may be locked behind these iron bars for a lifetime.

I would put in a plea, at this point, for the establishment of more dream analysis groups. The one-to-one method is, of course, immensely valuable and its worth has been established during the years since Freud's work began in Vienna, but this is, of necessity, very expensive in time and money, both for analyst and analysand. Dream groups were established in the first place 'faute de mieux' – better than nothing – for people aware of locked-up energy or the symptoms of anxiety, which arise in this condition. These groups, however, now proliferating, are not only economical, but they provide *holding* for the individual by the other group members. It becomes safe to let the dangerous creature break the bars of the cage. Childish tantrums can now be held in check, no longer by mother, but by the maturity of the dreamer, reinforced by the group – what he feared, he is reassured, is common to us all. When it emerges from the unconscious and comes into consciousness, it will submit to reason and become a source of greater energy in our everyday life.

*(1967)*

If thou couldst empty thyself of self
Like to a shell dishabited
Then might He find thee on the ocean shelf
And say "This is not dead"
And fill thee with Himself instead
But thou art all replete with very thou
And hast such shrewd activity
That when He comes He says, "This is enow
Unto itself – T'were better let it be,
It is so small and full there is no room for Me"

Isle of Man poet – *Brown*

# Resentment

What day is it? Tuesday, 12th September 1967: I was 82 last month on the 21st which is the last day of Leo and Leo's children set out on life, so they say, with courage and fiery determination. It takes this now to start my book which 'They' have been saying for long enough I should – I ought – to write. 'Ought' is a strong word spoken by super-ego forces in our lives. Jehovah spoke it from the mountain when he set out to discipline unruly slaves into a nation. "Thou shalt" he said, and "Thou shalt not".

Why did I not start earlier? There have been starts during the last year or more, a few pages written but the 'ought' was not strong enough to keep me going. Noel Carrington came to visit me last summer with his wife Catharine. I took them to see the Clinic and later I read to them some of what I had written. Noel has been a publisher and said, "Yes, go on. It *ought* to be written. You had never conveyed to us before what a place this Davidson Clinic is, nor what work you have been doing here. You must write". The secret, he said, was to set aside, if possible, two hours daily and let nothing intervene. Yes, well then let it lie till these two hours became possible. Yesterday was Monday, a day on which one *ought* to begin but yesterday was already booked by patients at 10 a.m., 11 a.m., 12 noon, 2 p.m., 3 p.m., 4 p.m., and by 5 p.m. my energy would have been caught up in the analytic process of concentration on the story, or on the emotional state of the patient.

At 10 a.m. the patient mostly screamed with rage at the total inadequacy of her home, her parents, her educators and now her analyst. I listened pretty dumbly, but sent her away with some tenderness hoping that all this vehement discharge of fury would clear the channels for a more ordered flow of creative energy. At 11 a.m. it was an orderly, happy, contented woman who had come originally because of her grief at her husband's sudden death. She had always thought longingly of analysis as she was aware of its liberating effect on others whom she knew. She came willingly, no 'ought' in her attendance. She 'wanted' to come, she wants to dream. Her hours with me are happy, easy hours. Sometimes she weeps, often we laugh together but there is increase of tranquillity in her life and already other people in her circle and beyond are benefiting from the development of her psyche. Today we talk for a time about conscious things – what she had done, whom she had met at the weekend, how perfect the weather is and "the air like silk". Yes, she had been dreaming but it seemed valueless, however here it was: "A couple of cartons had been deposited on my doorstep. I had not expected them and when I opened them they contained a large variety of trinkets. I discarded most of them but two seemed worth my consideration – a flexible bracelet that was ticketed 25 guineas, and a set of three rings, two jewelled, but the third perhaps platinum. It was like the modern fashionable wedding rings, rather broad, but the strange thing is that it was expandable. I was not happy about the three rings, insufficient room on my finger below the knuckles, and search as I would I could not find a tag denoting the price."

"What price a new wedding-ring?" I suggested. Since no subject is taboo on the analyst's couch, we talked about this, about woman's need of man and the price she has to pay if she becomes his slave. She felt happy to have opened up the subject. I felt grateful for "the air like silk".

Twelve o'clock – "I am late – it was difficult to get the baby off my hands." Perhaps the young mothers who for one reason or another come to me are, of all my patients, the most valuable and to be desired. Each human being has obviously great potential and each one whom we help to live with less anxiety and more energy is creative in his or her own right, and sets more doors open through which men and women can enter the Kingdom. By this I mean that they discover their own capacity for relationship, they have at their disposal the energy needed for work and find access to their creative gifts, the talents so often latent and unexploited.

My twelve o'clock patient found herself some months ago suddenly unable to focus in one eye and strangely weak on one side of her body. Her family doctor called in a consultant. She was taken to hospital and investigated in the modern manner. All the systems of bodily activity were examined in great detail and with scientific exactitude, but no one asked the necessary question, "Why did you fall ill?" She was discharged free from symptoms, but her husband was told that they would recur within a year and that a wheeled chair would be her probable fate within an unspecified time. As her husband and she lived within a church-going religious community they sought help through a minister friend whom they trusted, hoping that an intercession circle would enrol her on their prayer-list. They were rather taken aback when, instead, he suggested a visit to the Davidson Clinic. The patient wrote asking me to see her, told me of the diagnosis, and said she would like to know why she had got ill.

I had, strangely enough, wanted very much to analyse such a case. Once previously a woman in her fifties had come to me for a short time suffering from disseminated sclerosis. The condition was well-established and I undertook her treatment with very limited optimism. She remained relatively free of symptoms while she was with me but she had no expectation of recovery. I thought at the time that the secondary gains of her illness were a factor in her lack of interest in the possibility of recovery. Her husband and daughters were of necessity 'devoted' as long as she was an invalid.

My present patient, Ann, is very different. She herself wrote to ask for an investigation into the psychological factors behind her illness. At first she had no hope of 'cure' and often referred to "my disease". She had no symptoms when first I saw her so that I was able to ask, "At present is your body quite well and strong?", and to get a quick response, "Yes, I feel quite fit". I explained to her my idea that any illness which has remissions has also the possibility of cure, that is to say, the remission may be expected to last indefinitely in favourable circumstances. Gradually the sadness in her face disappeared, and we established a good rapport in analysis, and a matter-of-fact attitude towards her life, the relationships with husband, children, grandparents and friends occupying the focus of attention and the symptoms remaining in abeyance.

I had advised against involvement in situations of stress, such as sharing a holiday with difficult in-law connections, but my advice was not taken. She emerged triumphant since her husband and all other adults had been laid low by some virus infection, she alone had not succumbed. (She has not yet read Groddeck's *Book of the It*, but has quite a Groddeckian attitude to illness.) I often point out to her and to all my patients how our very language in talking of illness discloses the unconscious truth. We use the active not the passive voice, 'I have caught a cold', 'I have picked up a germ,' 'I have slipped a disc' – this latter being in the present fashion. One old farmer's wife, a friend of long ago, I remember came to see us with a swollen face and explained, 'I have stung myself with a bee.'

To sting oneself with a bee may seem farcical, but it illustrates an aspect of reaction between the body, – we call it the soma nowadays, – the psyche, and the environment. When the psyche becomes afraid, the soma secretes excessive adrenalin to prepare it to combat the aggressor. If the environment supplies a bee, it is stimulated by the odour in the breath or skin secretion to attack. Some 'bee people' who handle swarms and hives can do so without fear, need no protective clothing, excrete no excess of adrenalin, and the bees don't sting them. 'Psychosomatic' – Aubrey Lewis in his recently published book *The State of Psychiatry and Inquiries into Psychiatry* (Routledge 1967), wishes this word a transitory life and says that it reflects only a rather muddled phase of specialised ignorance. I agree to the extent of saying that to label *some* illnesses psychosomatic is evidence of our ignorance, but to be sure that in *all* illness there are psychological factors is to be wise.

The Davidson Clinic has been in action for twenty-seven years, and it is twenty-four years since I relinquished my private consulting room in Alva Street, but yesterday a telephone conversation took me back to visualise a scene in that room only partly forgotten. The telephone voice said, "You won't remember me but I had one or two talks with you some years ago." We went on to unravel the story. His wife had been a patient of mine all that long time ago. "Yes, " I said, "I remember, and often have wondered about her. How is she now?" "Oh, she is a complete invalid with rheumatoid arthritis. I had to give up my work and find a job where I could give her more attention." Recently a young American social worker told me that she had got a research job investigating the psychological cause of rheumatic illnesses. "Resentment every time," I remarked, in accordance with my habit of oversimplification. She looked suitably impressed and asked whether I had been reading recent American literature where, she said, they called it "repressed hostility". Good enough, I thought, subjectively, I know it as resentment – objectively they label it aggression which with its repressions covers whole chapters in the understanding of human life.

So now I bring back the memory of this family situation and some aspects of the relationship I had with this patient twenty-five years ago. Mary was the only daughter of important and wealthy people of the town. In marrying her, an insignificant but good looking young civil servant had thought he was making a good marriage. The bride's parents bought the young couple a house in very close proximity to their own – I visualised it as literally in the shadow of the big house. The daughter now acquiring a husband had thought she would be happy, independent, mistress of her own establishment. Her mother had quite other ideas although probably she was not entirely conscious of them and certainly would not put them into words. The words, had they been available, were: "I have acquired a son. I shall boss him as well as my daughter. I will keep them close, and by subsidising their income with my wealth make sure of their devotion."

As an only child Mary had suffered all her life from the anxiety of her parents. All their eggs, after all, were in one basket. Children do not thrive well in such an atmosphere, maternal anxiety is a substitute for love. Had you enquired tactfully and indirectly about the mother's love relationship with Mary you might have elicited the answer, "Yes, she is very dear to me. I am constantly anxious about her well-being." Mother and child worked themselves into each other's patterns, Mary often ailing, Mother finding much to worry about, many illnesses, much doctoring, a symbiosis only partially useful to the mother, destructive to the child whose goal is now set. Her husband's telephone message twenty-five years later confirms it: "I have had to give up my work and find a job where I could give her more attention".

But thinking sadly of this family disaster, I begin to remember more clearly my involvement in it. Mary's husband had "by chance" heard me speak at a meeting in Edinburgh on the subject of nervous illness and of family situations dominated by anxiety. His wife, he recognised, was "a nervous wreck", so he found his way to consult me and be assured that this condition was one in which analysis could be used hopefully. He was not at all sure that he could persuade her to put herself under my care as they lived at some distance from Edinburgh.

Her aunt, sister of her mother, lived in this town and after a good deal of urging, and I think also quarrelling, she gave in to giving this treatment a trial and came to live with this relative. She did not come because she *wanted* to be helped but in response to her husband's demand. He was by this time very impatient with her neurotic claims upon his time and attention, and had made her angry with his reiterated "It's high time you saw Dr. Rushforth". She sacrificed nothing to come: the parents paid the fees although they distrusted this new-fangled treatment and were probably also anxious about what picture Mary would paint of them once she got going. The resentment, which primarily belonged to the parental situation, found expression in her hostile attitude to me and led to this incident which I had often recalled and, indeed, used to illustrate how dramatically insight may flash into the analytic situation. So here is the story.

Mary walked into my consulting room one morning and before lying down on the couch she confronted me holding out her hands for inspection. "I don't mind your not making me better" she said, "I never thought you would. I do mind you making me wor-r-rse. My left hand has been bad for some time, but since I came to you last week my right hand is bad too. Look!" Indeed, the knuckles were swollen and no doubt painful. I responded with sympathy, but then said to her that undoubtedly she was reacting to treatment and that, although at present this was negative and distressing, still if we could analyse the situation it would yield material through which change could occur in a more positive direction. She was still hostile and sulky but lay down on the couch and did express something of her hostility for the husband who had been so keen to get her away from home for this treatment. Before she left I showed her my hand and told her that I had a knuckle which sometimes swelled and gave me pain. Invariably I could refer this to resentment and had to ask myself the question, "Who are you up against now, you stupid woman?" She had a look at my hand and could verify the non-arthritic state of my knuckles.

The next day she arrived in a very different mood, held out her hands and said they were not painful. "It is my turn to tell the story," she said. "You know I am staying with my aunt? She is just like my mother, a very domineering woman. One day last week when I was setting off to see you she said, 'Take your umbrella.' I objected but she insisted. As I left your room that day it was raining, but I was just like a child. I didn't put up the umbrella, preferring to get wet. But I was *clutching it tightly with my right hand* and next morning it was swollen." "Stress reaction," would be the scientist's explanation; "increase of resentment" was mine.

Sad to relate, this moment of insight was not followed up. The aunt and she proved too much for each other, and the dangers of self-disclosure made her decide to return home and I have neither seen nor heard of her till today.

Analysis is a long-term policy and it is questionable whether we analysts have any right to take on short-term patients who do not promise to commit themselves for at least a year or so. Personally I have never insisted on such commitment and although many of my patients do stay for years, yet with others a few talks, based analytically, have greatly changed their lives. Only this year a woman returned to tell me that she had had five sessions with me seventeen years ago which had profoundly altered the course of her life. We had not been in touch since, but now she felt I could help her again. Once a man on a bus asked me if I remembered him. "Yes, I don't forget my patients." In the time of a short journey he told me that an exhibition of paintings had been held recently which he thought I should have seen. After ten sessions with me he had not only begun to paint himself but started painting-groups in boys' clubs which had made a difference to quite a lot of people. This exhibition had been the result. I never saw him again, but I like to think that a stone thrown into a pool has ripples that spread.

*(1967)*

And a voice came to me, saying:
In every creature, in forest and ocean in leaf and tree and bird and breast and man, there moves a spirit other than its mortal own,
Pure, fluid, as air – intense as fire,
Which looks abroad and passes along the spirits of all other creatures, drawing them close to itself,
Nor dreams of other law than that of perfect equality;
And this is the spirit of immortality and peace.

And whatsoever creature hath this spirit, to it no harm may befall:
No harm can befall, for wherever it goes it has its nested home, and to it every loss comes charged with an equal again;
It gives – but at the hands of love;
And death is the law of its eternal growth.

"Towards Democracy", *Edward Carpenter*

# Responsibility

'She' was very indignant, really angry at what seemed my lack of sensitivity, when I suggested that the responsibility for her illness must be hers. I had spoken spontaneously: perhaps the words came unconsidered straight from the unconscious. Whatever their origin, I had better have a look at them. Truth has seven sides. Was her indignation a sign that I had hit upon one aspect, hidden or only partly conscious?

An angry reaction is one deserving of our attention – it has awakened feeling that we find unacceptable and tend to reject. I, too, had kept the idea only vaguely in my mind. It was not entirely acceptable to me in regard to this patient. Poor thing! I thought of her childhood, conditioned by maternal anxiety, which shielded her from contact with other children. She was too precious to be sent to school until she was over fourteen. An inadequate governess had taught her little. She covered her inadequacy when she reached school by 'playing the fool'. She could attract attention by her wit. Mutual dislike with her close mates saddened her school days. She made no real friends – a pattern which was still operating in her adult life.

So again the question – is she responsible for her illness? It is easier to put the blame on the parents, but were they responsible for their protective anxiety? As we traced the conditions back through the generations as we could see them, we could only surmise that she was the end product in a long family history of anxious, insecure people.

Was then her illness inevitable? Apparently this was not the case. There had been four members of the family and two of them were reported by the family doctor, who knew them well, to be 'perfectly normal people'. Only my patient and one sister had reacted by developing neurotic symptoms sufficiently obvious to attract attention. Further enquiry led to the observation that my patient and her sister were the oldest, followed by two boys. The boys had been sent to the village school and from there on to a boarding school where they had learned to be tough and had escaped from the anxiety of the parental home.

Consciously, of course, my patient was in no way responsible. No one in their senses would choose to suffer as she did. What purpose then did her illness serve? I recalled an old saying, 'There is a certain pleasure in being miserable'. The masochist, strangely isolated from his fellows, resorts to misery to bring some sort of interest into his life. 'Attention-seeking' is a notable symptom in ill-health. Failing in achievement of any creativity in life, do we find a substitute in becoming a centre of pity and interest through the destructive acceptance of illness? We see many contributing factors, then, in the need to fall ill, but let us recognize that creative activity is its best prevention.

How then can this happen in our lives – the liberation of creativity? Fear and anxiety are its great enemies, stifling it at the source, but the spirit of love gives us hope. 'Love casts out fear.' As we mutter the Lord's Prayer let us expect an answer to our petitions. 'Deliver us from evil' meets with the answer that in Christ Jesus is freedom. Let us accept it in the fullness of its meaning – and know Christ the liberator in all life's problems.

'She', of course, is sure that it is God who sends His illness upon her and gives this as a good reason for not trusting in Him to keep everything in her life smooth and easy. 'Before I was afflicted I went astray but now have I kept the Word' gives a positive value to the idea that God sends us our afflictions – illness, accident, bereavement – be what they may.

Early in my analytic work I had been warned not to expect a 'cure' in a manic-depressive patient, and with this warning also perhaps went some scorn at anyone who would undertake the onus of treating such a person. By substituting the idea of *care* for that of *cure* it becomes feasible to undertake such cases. In caring, however, the possible outcome of *healing* presents itself. Both analyst and patient hope and long for such an outcome.

Looking again at the theory underlying the analytic process, we recollect that its aim is to free the patient from the painful conditions of the past by bringing into consciousness the feeling repressed because of the pain, fear or guilt attached to it. Once conscious, the matter can be dealt with rationally – whereas reason does not operate in the unconscious. But how can this be accomplished? It's like raising a corpse from the sea bottom if a cannon ball is firmly attached to its feet. Get all the help you can! Facts that have emerged from our work together are: -

1. She is afflicted with self-loathing. No-one, she believes, is as evil as she.

2. From this we deduce that she is a very special person – no one can compete.

3. She has a great need to be 'special' in other ways: my special friend.

4. She is completely self-centred. Every sentence begins with 'I' and whoever comes into the conversation must give way to her experience.

5. She awakes in the night panic-stricken, but the cause of the panic is inaccessible (cannon-ball?)

Asking for help brought me a letter from Maurice Kidd in London, begging me to follow up Fairbairn and Guntrip in their idea that such a patient prefers to be strong and miserable, to being weak and happy! (Does he not realise my age? – but he has come to my help.) For strong substitute 'important' and for miserable 'depressed'. I can recognise her as a very important depressed person. She never stops telling me how unimportant she is but is this the cause of panic? It may be true that she is unimportant! Can she face the reality of this? We have already noted the 'certain pleasure' of misery. Is she clinging to this rather than facing herself as she is with plenty of undeveloped potential that she can't/won't use? By facing it would she cut the cords of that cannon-ball?

Choice is a human prerogative. Is it possible that 'She' will choose to allow the memory at present so destructive in its repression to come into her consciousness. Liberated, the corpse could come to the surface and undoubtedly something would happen!

*(1979)*

# The Mask

Let us consider how the personality, even in early development, protects itself against influences that may hurt it, such as parental condemnation or the disapproval of others. A child, early in his life, becomes aware that conformity to parental ideas earns him his parents' approval, while disobedience or unwillingness to submit to their ideas lands him in a situation of conflict. Let us visualise ourselves as set between two worlds, with 'I am', the conscious ego, situated in the centre. The world of the outer influences comprises, in the first place, the parents, family, teachers, neighbours and ultimately, conventional society. We think of this, and frequently dream of it, as belonging to the right-hand side and call it by the Freudian term 'superego'. The words it speaks are 'You ought' and associated with it is Yahweh, the God of the Old Testament with his commands 'Thou shalt' and 'Thou shalt not'. I can remember clearly in my childhood being assured by my pious parents that God did not love disobedient, 'naughty' children; in this way they justified their own attitude towards the rebellious or self-willed child.

In order to protect ourselves against disfavour we assume the mask, the false face, which bears the brunt of the adversely critical forces and averts undue hurt from the conscious ego. In psychological teaching the concept of the mask or 'persona' is one of great importance. All of us wear masks. Children adopt them in their play. In older forms of drama, in ancient Greece or classical Oriental theatre, masks were worn on stage to express the character portrayed by the actor. Surgeons wear masks when in contact with an open wound to prevent infection being conveyed to the patient.

Ideally our persona should, as it were, be light, with the possibility of keeping it on or taking it off. When, however, the superego forces are harsh the mask becomes impervious, no longer easily handled but fixed like a visor protecting the face. I would emphasise that this process begins very early in life, even in infancy. Human beings cannot exist without the persona, the face they present to the world and are largely judged by whether the mask makes for agreeable relationships or fends off oncoming friends. It is important to realise that whilst initially the superego is externally represented by the parents and others ('They say this is how I ought to behave.') we proceed to internalise it and say 'I know what is expected of me. I ought to do such and such.' The well-behaved child and the agreeable adult accept what society has brought into being. Much is obviously gained through this attitude, but much also can be lost if self-will is entirely abandoned in favour of other people's demands. The doormat personality emerges in cases of people who are downtrodden and willing to have other's demands and ideas operative rather than their own. Such people are uncreative and suffer much humiliation. Self-will, knowing what we want, is essential for the good life but the necessity of balance or compromise must not be forgotten.

These superego forces, originating in the discipline of early life, have to meet the instinctual forces, which we call 'libido' or 'id' and which we can visualize as coming from the left-hand side and the heart. These libidinous forces have their origin in the depth of our being, the unconscious. Just as with the superego we have postulated Yahweh, so now in the origin of all things we postulate the creative source of our lives and energy, and of the Universe, which we call God. The words of the unconscious, operating through our instinctual lives are 'I need' and 'I want'. From infancy instincts are apparent. Being born is associated with fear, a primitive instinct, but if good contact is made with the mother's breast, love, instinctively present in the unborn, develops.

Between these two worlds, then, lies the conscious ego. It is easy to understand that conflicts always exist between 'I ought' and 'I want'; that is to say between the superego forces and those of the libido; and the libido, deriving as it does its energy from the deep unconscious, has a strength greater than that of the contrary forces derived from civilisation. Yahweh, the God of the Israelites, still wields his power as of old but mankind has come to understand him as a God of Love. The will of God and the love of God, since the coming of Christ, can be known and understood to be always for man's highest good.

In the Book of Revelation we are taught that a great river flows from the throne of God into the lives of men and women. Can we now change our picture from a two dimensional surface with right-hand and left-hand sides and make it instead into a sphere where Yahweh and God, the source of our instinctual energy, are seen to be parts of one being? If this is so, then the law, understood as discipline in man's life, need not be separated from the love which creates.

Thinking again of our two dimensional representation of the personality, with psychic energy symbolised as entering on the left-hand side, we could envisage the energy of our being as electricity; an electro-magnetic force emanating from the Ground of All Being which is beyond our comprehension. As it enters the individual it must accommodate itself to the capacity for usefulness. Destruction would be inevitable were the flow of cosmic energy not somehow controlled and mitigated. We can visualise some kind of transformer, functioning in the same way as the transformer which lies between a torrent of mountain water, the driving force for hydro-electric power and the house or factory where the electric energy is eventually used. In our model, we can see this 'transformer' as situated to the left of the ego, in which position it balances the persona on the right. Energy must constantly be transmitted into the living creature; without it life would cease. The optimum use of this energy as a spiritual force is what now concerns us.

Each individual person is a channel of creative energy and hence, each has enormous possibilities. What is it that enables some of us to be so much more available and full of energy than others. in terms of giving our lives creativity and usefulness? This must lie in the degree of openness of the channel through which the energy of life passes. It is as if the power is always available, but the channels not always open for it to pass through. Saint Theresa of Avila assured us of God's need for each of us as a channel for his power: "God has no hands but man's hands, no feet but man's feet.". We can see ourselves as co-creative with the eternal purpose, with immense potential, but with great differences as to how we receive the energy and pass it on into the world outside.

Can each of us see ourselves as having the function of taking creative energy from the source, holding it in our being in everyday life and always being able to give it again wherever it is demanded of us and needed? So often we hear the bitter complaint of tiredness and lack of energy, but the energy can be renewed from the source. It is always available, sometimes to our surprise, even when a demand is made. The good life involves this taking, holding and giving again, which gives us an awareness of the flow and makes us able to serve our purpose in the divine scheme of things.

The work of psychoanalysis is one form of an attempt to open the channels and to release the energy from the repression of the superego, making it available where it is needed. There are other methods, of course, such as the spiritual teachings and transpersonal therapies which lead us to a better knowledge of the Self and of our ability to act as channels for the love and power of God.

*Editors' Note*: Although for the most part Dr. Rushforth spoke of analysis as the royal, or indeed the only road to self-knowledge, she did acknowledge that conventional analysis, in the terms of a medically-trained psychiatrist working with a patient several times a week for a year or more was unrealistic today. She did not work quite as formally as this herself, and Dr. Rushforth in her later years became interested in the wide range of new techniques practiced by counsellors and psychotherapists, to help their clients more rapidly achieve personal insights. She was particularly interested in her daughter's work, at Wellspring, in Edinburgh; here short and longer term clients are assisted in various ways, including the person-centred technique of Dr. Eugene Heimler's Human Social Functioning. As the last paragraph above indicates, Dr. Rushforth insisted that those techniques that had an implicit spiritual bias were far more valuable than those which did not.

(1983)

# The Basic Instincts

Some years ago I was asked to take part in a religious broadcast arranged by Scottish Television. There were six participants talking about the Sermon on the Mount as recorded in the Gospel of St. Matthew. I was accorded first choice. On what words would I like to speak? "Murder, please." My interviewer, greatly relieved, thanked me, saying that no one else was likely to choose the words.

Three categories of guilt, three grades of punishment, are mentioned. Murder? Well, let us realise how often the thought of this disposal of the irritating, troublesome relative, friend, neighbour, springs to expression. 'I could murder that brat' in the mouth of adoring parents. 'I wish he were dead', then a way might open without frustration. Our Lord's teaching equates murder with anger, perhaps saying 'Watch yourself. Be aware of your anger.' The second category denotes a condescending attitude, superiority. We attain our own righteousness by putting the other in the wrong. The third, renegade in modern translation, has to do with religious practice. Later the parable of the Pharisee and the publican casts light on this attitude – the holy man, arrogant and unaware that he is in need of God's forgiving mercy compared to the other, who accepts his guilt but is aware that he can be forgiven.

Look then at the three categories of judgement. Murder, strangely enough, is not condemned as the worst form of wickedness. The murderer, the irritated, angry, violent man, must be taken to task 'in the village court' – that is, by his fellows. No punishment is inflicted but he is warned, it may be not even urged to change his ways, but rather to be conscious, aware, to realise what effect anger has in relationship. Then the Sanhedrin, the High Court in Jerusalem, to this court which condemned our Lord to death, is sent the man who calls his brother 'Fool'. Perhaps the meaning might be that society cannot approve of the superiority-inferiority attitude, so destructive to brotherliness, equality, and feelings of commonality. Another aspect of this is that 'superior people' are also condemned to their own inferiority in the scale of being. 'All men are equal in the sight of God' – knowing this we would cease from arrogance and the striving to go one better.

Now to go back to the STV recording – my interviewer was a Christian minister and seemed somewhat uneasy about what I might present to the unknown, uncounted audience. The cameras were already prepared to focus on us when he said anxiously, "But after all you must admit that anger is a base instinct". I had only time to rejoin "No, no, not base, basic".

In the scale of evolution the aeon stretches back into infinity. We may picture humanity as the budding, flowering, fruiting and seeding of the great Tree of Life. We can only guess how it was propagated in the good earth and began to grow. Where did the seed come from? What preparation was necessary of the stony ground to receive the seed and give it the opportunity? Each germinating individual made it easier for his fellow to find a niche for development. Infinite patience, long drawn out slow development – in duration, not yet in time. Rooted downward, its stem reaches upward and bears leaves, then flowers and fruits and again the seed.

Earlier still, something was alive in the sea, mobile though not equipped with fins, sponge-like – taking, holding, giving again the seawater and so maintaining life. In evolution something is always happening and in this passage (the second category) we learn to give encouragement to our brother who is struggling with his inferiority, his self-abasement. 'Thou Fool' drives him further into despair, but knowing him as brother, according to him equality, neither to be envied nor despised, we can find our path, hand in hand on life's highway.

The third category in which mankind is judged and for which the punishment is hellfire, relates to the parable of the Pharisse and the publican. The Pharisee masks his lack of love and caring with the good deeds which involve the outer rather than the inner life. He makes no effort to share the humility and self-abasement of the other, whose whole consciousness is focussed on God as merciful and his own need of mercy and forgiveness. Had the Pharisee not in the end found himself in Hell? To maintain his false righteousness must have been a hellish business, like teetering on the brink of a precipice in constant danger of falling to his death.

The instinctual life, the basic instincts, are a part of human

equipment with which man is endowed. His life flourishes or wilts
in proportion to how fully he is able to live by their guidance,
without the fear of their power to dominate him. They are basic,
not base, whether anger, sex, mother love, curiosity or any of the
other urges recognised in our behaviour. Freud subsumed all the
instincts as either creative, life-giving, or destructive death-
dealing. They constitute the great motivating force in animal and
human life. We recognise them in the early 'I want', as the child
acquires speech, but earlier they are in the unspoken 'I need' of the
infant. With life-maturity, 'I want' becomes 'I am willing' and
ultimately we surrender ourselves to 'That' greater than ourselves,
which brings us into conformity with Life's purposes and gives us
peace.

(1980)

Let your mind be quiet
Realising the beauty of the world and the immense and boundless
      treasures that it holds for you.
All that you have within you,
All that your heart desires,
All that your nature so specially fits you for,
That, in the counterpart of it
Waits embedded in the great Whole for you.
It will surely come to you. Yet equally surely,
Not one moment before its appointed time will it come.
All your crying and fever and reaching out of hands, will make no
      difference.
Therefore do not begin that game at all.
Do not recklessly spill the waters of your mind in this direction
      or that,
Lest you become like a spring lost and dissipated in the desert.
But draw them together into a little compass
And hold them still – so still –
And let them become clear – so clear – so limpid – so mirror-like.
At last the mountains and the skies shall clasp themselves in
      peaceful beauty
And the antelope shall descend to drink and to gaze at his reflected
      image
And the lion shall quench his thirst
And love himself shall come and bend over and catch his reflected
      image in you.

"A Meditative Poem" – Edward Carpenter

# Dream Reality

At the first Summer School held twenty-three years ago, our guest lecturer, Dr. Kathleen Landon, drew on a blackboard a map of the Psyche in which she indicated that the Ego, that is you or I, as we are conscious of our being, live in a state of tension between two worlds designated 'The World of Outer Reality' and 'The World of Inner Reality'. Since I had previously lived for twenty years in India I was aware that Vedic thought also postulated two worlds, that of Maya-Illusion which is identified with the world as we know it – things, places, people, matter, space, time – but that in the Vedic philosophy the true life is the life of the spirit, not imprisoned in these dimensions. In my early life I found it difficult, almost ridiculous, to deny the reality of the things we touch and see. Life, however, changes as we grow older. Jung tells us that we pass the watershed at about 35, and thereafter the spiritual world begins to acquire more reality, and to define itself with more certainty in our *consciousness* as we age and mature.

The dream comes from the world of 'Inner Reality' of which we are so largely unconscious in ordinary waking life. It is indeed the easiest way of contact, breaking through from sleep into waking life. The great analytic schools were founded on dream analysis, and although Freud and Jung differ in their methods of interpretation, both depend on the dream, and its ability to lure the dreamer into the mysterious depths of his nature.

From the days of our childhood all, I suppose, have been interested and curious, 'intrigued', with the subject of dreams. I can remember resenting the fact that Bible days were different from present days in that angels no longer appeared to me, or to anyone I knew personally, in a dream. I envied Joseph his talent of dream interpretation. This is possibly a factor in my interest and devotion to the recording and interpretation of dreams as described by Freud and Jung, and other writers, and my present day involvement in analytical psychotherapy in which the dream, as a medium of communication between analyst and analysand, is of such great importance.

Until quite recently, the last ten years or so, *dreaming* was only known as a subjective experience, and to-day, although *dreaming* has been the object of scientific observation and research, still it is true that *the dream* is a subjective experience, and to what extent it can be communicated is a matter of guess-work.

I would like to recapitulate briefly, and certainly inadequately, some account of the modern knowledge of the dream process. A student in Chicago, working on the process of sleep and waking in new-born babies, observed that at certain stages of sleep, *rapid eye movements* occured behind the closed eyelids and he asked the question, "Can this be associated with dreaming?" What a simple observation and what a simple question! The elucidation could be carried out by the use of the electroencephalograph discovered and elaborated in Britain during the last forty years (since the Kaiser war). By attaching electrodes to the scalp the electric currents set up in the brain can be amplified and recorded graphically – these are the brain waves.

By taking these E.E.G. records during the sleeping hours a correlation between them and the rapid eye movements (the R.E.M.) was established – a change in the recorded brain-waves preceding the R.E.M. By awakening the sleeper at this juncture it was discovered that it almost invariably coincided with a dream. By recording the total night's sleep it then became plain that sleep fell into at least two categories – deep dreamless sleep, and a lighter sleep in which dreams occur associated with R.E.M., and other physiological changes (muscle relaxation, quickened respiration and pulse). More-over, a cyclic pattern of dreaming is *universal*, and an objective distinction can be made between the dreaming and non-dreaming phases of sleep. Three stages of brain activity are – waking, deep sleep, and dreaming sleep.

Each of us knows from experience that prolonged loss of sleep causes us to be less efficient and more irritable in the work-a-day world. In laboratory conditions men and women volunteer for prolonged periods of sleeplessness, and suffer from great impairment of function. Humans cannot be allowed to suffer more than a limited deprivation, although this has occured in the brainwashing torture, but animals have died as a result of sleep-deprivation carried out ruthlessly.

It is now established that the dream-bearing sleep is necessary for mental health. After a period of total wakefulness the subject, when allowed to sleep, falls into this dream-sleep almost continuously. He makes up for the loss of dreams with more urgency than for the loss of deep sleep. Small children spend more of the 24 hours in the third (dream-bearing) state than adults, but in old age it may again pre-dominate. Children we know are interested, and want to understand. I can testify that this same curiosity persists and recurs in old age when the irrational mystic occurrences not only of dreaming, take us again into our childhood but also into areas beyond our cognition. Dr. Ian Oswald, of the research unit in Psychological Medicine in Edinburgh University, has discovered that in the third state there is evidence, in his male subjects, of rhythmic sexual upsurge as a normal occurrence. In this third state the cerebral cortex is excluded from functioning, and the primitive instinctual sexual urges can assert themselves and be recorded, thus corroborating Freud's theories of sexuality.

Freud called the Dream, "the royal road to the unconscious" an honour, which in these days, it may well share with the *symptom* of an illness. When patients have learned to be responsible for their dreams they can then be persuaded to take a similar attitude to their illnesses. At first when I was learning to practise analysis many of my patients were uneducated people, and I made a practice of asking them, "Who gave you the dream?" or, "Where did the dream come from?" The answer was quite probably, "I suppose God sent it", or, "Perhaps it was due to indigestion". "No, no!" I would say, "*You* made it! It's *your* dream! Let us try and see what *you* are saying in this story".

Freud wrote concerning dreams at the turn of the century, and his 'interpretation' has been held for more than sixty years to be a work of genius. From him we learn to look in the dream-content for some aspect of repressed instinctual drive, and to ask in what way does this dream postulate the fulfilment of a wish. Possibly Dr. Ian Oswald's work, as noted above, has bearing on this aspect of Freud's theories. In the dream-sleep (third state) we are free from the influence of the cerebral cortex which is that part of our brain which makes us specifically human – it enables us to think, to reflect, to regret and to anticipate, to make decisions and to choose our path; but more than this it is the organ of restraint. C.S. Sheldon, the American writer, in describing the different categories of temperament – viscero-tonic, somato-tonic and cerebro-tonic – states that the cerebro-tonic individual is, above all, noted for this capacity to hold back, to restrain. More than one little boy, in the days when they said their prayers at bed-time, would begin, "Please God bless Father and Mother", and would end up, "and please don't let the boiler burst". Even educated and cultured women I have met, have a secret phobia that the cistern controls will lose their efficacy, or that the thermostat of the boiler will fail and the boiler explode. In these cases symbolism has asserted itself even in waking life, but floods and overwhelming forces of sea, of fire and tempest are common in dreams. This indicates that the 'higher', cortical, restraining centres are out of action, and that the 'lower', more primitive, instinctual centres are free to express themselves. It is the *too* good child, *too* well behaved, *too* rigidly disciplined, *too* early under self-control who prays his little prayer about the boiler. In the same way the rigidly virtuous woman may well fear her primitive emotions breaking through into unconventional and unacceptable behaviour.

The scientists who are experimenting on animals observe that, in an animal whose cerebral cortex is destroyed, there is still evidence of dreaming in the R.E.M. and the electroencephalograph rhythmic changes. Freud's theory that the dream is wish-fulfilment is based on this breaking through of the instinctual life, the idle desires, the underlying animal aspect of humanity of which we are so apt to be ashamed. In the dream we do the most shocking and dreadful things without shame or distress: modest, shy ladies frequently find that the lavatory is open to all in the hotel drawing-room, and murders are committed without guilt.

Jung followed Freud but disagreed with him about the sexual and instinctual nature of the dream processes. If Freud discovered the unconscious as Christopher Columbus discovered America, Jung has been likened to Magellan or Champlain, the men who followed the rivers to their sources, and added much knowledge about the structure of the unconscious from which both postulate that the dream emerges.

A simplification of the Jungian theory, which is of great use in psychotherapy, is the statement, "Everyone in the dream is yourself". The dream provides a screen on which we project our images, men and women and children of all ages and races; houses, mansions, cottages, hotels, institutions; vehicles that travel on the sea, or land, or in the air; birds and fishes and beasts; trees and shrubs and flowers; weapons of offence and defence, armies of soldiers; choirs of innocent children; mountains and hills, firm land, stony land, boggy land; clouds, streams, great rivers, lakes and the sea. What an infinite variety of environment and strange assortment of persons! Perhaps it seems ridiculous to think that you and I can be so many-sided or live in such differing circumstances.

To leave the dream for a moment and think of our physical heredity. The geneticists tell us that you and I carry in our bodies, indeed in each cell of our bodies, the actual sub-microscopic units of our inheritance, the genes. If indeed Adam and Eve are our ancestors then in our bodies we have the very genes that Adam and Eve carried before they went to bed together to Make Cain and Abel. Similarly, in our unconscious, we carry the memory traces of our remote ancestry. It may be that the activity of the cerebral cortex does not allow them to function openly in the waking hours, but in the *third state*, the dreaming opportunity, there they are presenting themselves to our notice.

*Notice – pay attention – watch* these dreams with theur intimations of, not only immortality, but also of immorality – "Know thyself". Dark people come into our dreams, ranging from Indian rajahs to African slaves, but they are not necessarily disguised as foreign to ourselves. Very often the dark unknown presents himself as someone, usually of the same sex as the dreamer, whom we think of as an enemy – as bad, as disgusting, as beneath notice. Well, it is wise to take notice, and to see whether, by understanding this person, putting ourselves in his shoes, some light is not shed on our own personal attitudes and problems.

We dream of the dark continent, of China, Japan, or the Antipodes. These lands are symbolic of the deep unconscious. Newfoundland or North America I think often symbolises the newly discovered world which is opening up through analysis. I remember being encouraged when a difficult, recalcitrant patient, whom I sadly thought of as beyond my power to help, brought one day, instead of a dream, a painting which he said was a design for a postage stamp. It was an outline map of Australia but the caption was Newfoundland. I felt that the journeys we had made together, exploring the depths, were after all to be rewarded by new life, and such proved to be the case. His life became creative and he did much in the service of humanity.

What are the emotions most frequently depicted in dreams? I think we must answer anxiety, fear, panic. Psychologists teach us that fear is part of man's instinctual equipment necessary to preserve life. Anxiety derives from fear and the existentialists postulate that anxiety too is ontological, that is, it belongs to all individuals. The Bible contradicts this, I believe, with its constantly recurring, "Fear not", urging us to be aware of the presence of the other than human, the Creative comforting spirit always seeking its way in man.

Four-squareness and its nature is a recurrent theme in Jungian teaching, and this is a common visual picture in the dream. Four is a symbol of integration, and when we look out for it in dream pictures we find it surprisingly often – tennis-courts, swimming-pools, college quadrangles, market squares, castle courtyards, four actors on the stage. Recently a young business woman in her thirties came asking for help. Her conscious problem was an unsuccessful love affair, but more deeply an uncertainty about her own value, a difficulty in claiming what was her due. After seeing her twice, and discussing the more conscious difficulties, I suggested she watch for a dream, and this is what she brought me. "A sum of money was owing to me but I was muddled and confused about it. The sum seemed to be about £30 and the money was then lying on a table. suddenly it seemed as if a square frame surrounded it. As I watched this halved and halved again, and in each of the four compartments so formed lay an equal sum. The problem was solved."

A quick and superficial interpretation was:

About 30 – the *here and now* problem of her present age.
It is *on the table*, that is, it is conscious and it can be handled.
It is *framed*, it can be seen as a problem of individuation.
Solution – equality for self and others.

I am aware that different analysts would interpret this dream differently. My reaction was, "Wouldn't the wise old man" (this is what his disciples call Jung) "be delighted to think of an analysis beginning so hopefully?"

I would again assert that, in my experience of psychotherapy, the dream is indeed the royal road to healing. We cannot understand ourselves until we understand our dreams, we cannot forgive ourselves or others until we understand – "Tout comprendre c'est tout pardonner", and to know fogiveness is to be healed.

(*The Bulletin*, April 1967)

"Let go and let God" – and don't get in his way!

# Fulfilment in the Married Life of Women

Work published in recent years by Wilhelm Reich give us an interesting development of Freud's teaching. Life, he says, as it issues from the unconscious, divides into two main streams – one providing sexual energy and the other the necessary vigour for the work demanded of mankind. He shows us what crippling effect the fear and consequent repression of sex-energy has in our civilised life. We do not accept the postulate that life has its own controls, and we therefore constantly use up the energy that should go into work in repressing the stream of sexual energy. This accounts for much of the listlessness and asthenia of civilised men and women. When sexual energy is the vehicle of love it has its own control and balance. When, however it is the vehicle of cruelty it has destructive power and is rightly to be feared. The destiny of the individual and indeed of mankind is wrapped up in this question whether love or hate controls this vital stream.

We use our *sexuality* as a means of *relating* ourselves to others, the child relating to the mother, the man relating to the woman, and again the parents relating to the child.

A woman of necessity begins life as daughter and on entering marriage she finds her task is to leave this relationship behind her and enter into a new bond, that of mate, of wife to her husband. Later a fresh development takes place, she becomes the mother, and out of this again a fourth stage may emerge—that of the creative woman. Ideally these developments take place *in marriage* but not of necessity, since they are inherently latent in every woman's psyche, awaiting their opportunity to emerge. It is also true that they take place *in time* but not only in time. Each of us *is* everything past, present and, even in some way, future. The child rising five, not yet at school, may be the perfect little mother to the younger infants who play with her in some nursery or back street. In analytic work this idea of the unity of the individual from the time of conception through all stages of growth, with the gradual clarification of life's pattern, is of great significance. It is true to say we *are*, not we *were*, embryo, unborn child, babe, toddler, schoolgirl, teenager, and so on into old age.

Let us, however, return to the newly-married woman and watch her disentangling herself from the position of devoted daughter. Up till this time to be 'good' may have meant to be approved by her parents, to do nothing to alienate their regard, to modify her opinions to suit theirs. It may have meant that security lay in the parents' home and that freedom was limited by their anxiety as to her welfare. Often unmarried women long past their teens must still account for their time and report of their doings to their parents. This creates so close a bond that the daughter suffers intensely and is unable to break the relationship. Although consciously she yearns to leave home and resents the grip upon her, yet her unconscious sees to it that she falls ill rather than tear herself away. The fact of marriage does not itself break the tie but a process is initiated and gradually the truth dawns 'Daughter am I in my mother's house, but mistress in my own'. If this is not realised and the married woman lives as if her loyalty lay towards her own parents she has little chance of developing fully and truly into wife and mother.

The awakening of the daughter into her full womanhood is the subject of many legends and fairy tales, the Sleeping Beauty, for instance, who involves not only herself but her whole environment in her sleep. All the work of the palace comes to a standstill until she is awakened by the kiss of the Fairy Prince. The cause of the disaster and the occasion which excites it are worthy of notice. It was caused by the absence of a fairy from her christening. Was the fairy's name perhaps 'Wantedness'? It is possible that a son was wanted when she was born? This lack of welcome might well cause a blight to fall on her life. Children are extremely sensitive to the parents' disfavour if they are unwanted or not quite what was wanted. Then you remember the occasion of the sleep was the pricking of her finger which occurred in spite of all precautions. Unwanted children are often treated with undue precautions, fenced in lest disaster befall them. This seems to be due to the initial destructive feeling of the parents against the infant, afterwards over-compensated. The pricking of the finger is probably symbolic of the first menstruation. The adolescent whose infantile difficulties are unresolved tends to relive them with great intensity in her teens and the normal drawing back into herself is exaggerated so that all relationships become difficult or impossible—this is the sleep of the fairy tale. With the arrival of the Fairy Prince—if indeed he gets close enough to kiss her—the maiden awakes. The man sees his mate as the altogether lovely one and partly accepting, partly rejecting this vision of his, she is drawn towards him. 'Love is blind' they say, and the vision of perfection is sadly unreal. 'Love conquers all' is perhaps, however, a greater truth and when the self-love or egocentricity of the daughter and son gives way to mutual response carrying with it the desire to serve each other and fulfil the need of both, then daughter gives place to wife and son to husband.

The probability of the daughter developing happily into the wife is also tied up with the degree to which she has been satisfactorily related to both parents. The father as well as the mother is a necessity in the life of the child. In the triangle, father, mother, child, all building of personality takes place. Identification with the mother, an unconscious process, occurs first of all and very importantly at the breast. Then as the small daughter grows and is curious about her own body she may now wisely be taught that she is like Mummy and not like the boys and Daddy. When she comes to puberty 'we women' may be shown to have our privileges and duties as well as our mysteries and women's rights. Identification with the opposite sex, with the boys or the father, is often a cause of frigidity and consequent marital unhappiness.

The words *response* and *responsibility* are of importance in early married life. It is through making glad responses and welcoming responsibility that the strength of the marriage develops. Some time ago one of the medical journals published an article dealing with the effect of the shopping basket on a woman's shoulders. Since delivery vans went out of fashion women, it is said, have developed grave disorders affecting the shoulder joints. I cannot help thinking that the disorder is primarily one of the emotions. When the heavy basket causes resentment the whole posture will express that emotion, the body will sag and the burden will cause injury. When the heavy basket is a cause of rejoicing the shoulders will go back and the body will brace itself with pride and satisfaction to take home the food acquired with the output of ingenuity and resource.

The burden that is very heavy in marriage is the weight of the husband's disapproval. He has in his own mind an image of the perfect wife derived from the memory of his own young mother. He has married believing that 'she' will conform to this picture and of course she does no such thing. The danger is that she tries too hard to conform, so distorting her own personality, living up to his idea of her instead of living from her own centre.

And now wife into mother—more burdens and more responsibility offer themselves. To the child of the future the mother's attitude from the very first is of the greatest importance. The child who is desired, whose mother sings the Magnificat when she knows herself pregnant, is already well set on his way. It also matters to him and to the mother that the father too rejoices over the pregnancy and allies himself with it. Delight in the experience is a high-water mark affecting favourably all three lives. 'We are pregnant' or 'The family is pregnant' gives the attitude of the family circle closing in to give the infant his fundamental security. Should this opportunity be missed it is all too likely that the child comes to belong particularly to the mother, and there develops an attitude of two against one which in greater or less degree makes conflict in the family. During these years of early married life with the birth of children there are endless opportunities to break down old patterns and create new, to relate and re-relate to husband and children. Through this activity growth takes place and a fuller personality develops. Parenthood is a means of fulfilment rather than an end in itself.

The fourth stage of a woman's fulfilment is that of 'mater creatrix'. Her age may be known now not by the frailty of her body but by the strength and creativness of her spirit. In his book *Venture to the Interior*, Laurens van der Post gives a wonderful description of such a woman in his appreciation of his mother. "It has often occured to me that the heavy burden of bearing and rearing children—and my mother reared thirteen—has, in a sense, been irrelevant to the deepest and most vital purpose of her life. I have never been able to believe that a woman's task in life is limited to her children. I can well conceive that in my mother, as with more and more women of our day, there is an urge to creativeness which lies underneath and deeper, above and beyond the begetting of children. These women have a contract with life itself, which is not discharged by the mere procreation of their species. Men recognise and try to honour this contract in themselves but they do not acknowledge and respect the same thing so readily in women. Perhaps until they do the world will not see the full creative relationship that life intends there should be between men and women."

The Creative Spirit is ever seeking its way in mankind and the work of analytical psychotherapy is only fully justified when it issues in setting free the full creativity of men and women. Nicholas Berdyaev in his autobiography *Dreams and Reality* hints at our responsibility "God demands from man a daring creative response . . . the summit of daring is reached in the awareness that on man depends not human life alone but divine life." Nothing can be added to this except perhaps a humble prayer for integration and a bowing of the head towards the holy creative purpose.

*(From a lecture given at the Sempervivum Easter School, 1952)*

Nothing imperfect is:
Equal are gold, tin,
Frogs are as beautiful
as are the Seraphim.

From "The Cherubinic Wanderer," *Angelis Silesius*

# The Hidden Talent

In our common talk today we use the word Talent to denote a special gift. He has a talent for music, a talent for making friends, a talent for drawing the best out of children, for teaching and so on. Do we forget that the talent orginally was a silver coin of some value current in Palestine in the time of Jesus? We use the word today because of Jesus' symbolic use of the word in the Parable of the Talents.

Early in my childhood it was brought home to me that I had no gift for music ("poor child, just like her father") who certainly did not sing in tune, though I think he sang a lot spontaneously, if unappreciated, when he was happy. The idea of talent must have been frequently discussed, for quite early in life I assured my mother (who was a highly gifted pianist) that I would produce musical children!

In due course I married a man who was musically well endowed. He took a first class degree in mathematics at Cambridge and had an early intellectual grasp of diverse fields. Music, however was the gift which he used to enrich his own life and others. He had particular pleasure in accompanying singers, violinists, cellists and flautists. We had four children and it was not surprising that we expected them to inherit his musical gifts.

When our daughters were very small, three and two years old, my husband decided to teach himself the clarinet. At the time we had a somewhat prolonged holiday trekking in the hills beyond Simla in a leisurely way, resting for a few days at a time and moving on again, with plenty of time for relaxation. Clarinets produce strange sounds in their early contact with a learner, disapproved of by the elder daughter who wept noisily when he began. She was removed out of hearing but her sister wept bitterly when the hour was over! Both of them developed their musical gifts and learned to play cello and violin as well as the piano early in their schooldays Di, the younger sister, has her house full of different instruments with much music-making and riches of fellowship in the gifts she shares with friends.

The third in our family, our son Jock, was sent to learn the violin at quite a tender age, but after a few weeks the verdict of hopeless was given with the remark "You might as well teach a colour blind person to paint". However, nothing daunted and remarking that the piano is a fool-proof instrument, his father engaged a teacher of the then modern Chassevant method. After a few months the teacher reported "He is a very dear little fellow. I have taught him to play 'The Clockwork Train' but cannot get him interested in going further".

At the age of twelve Jock was now at a school where the director of music trained a choir and an orchestra. My husband and I visited them when the Messiah was produced and we noticed that Jock sang in the chorus and could be heard spontaneously singing and humming the airs. So my husband paid a visit to the musical director to ask that his son should be taught a woodwind instrument. "My dear Sir" was the response "Your son is completely unmusical". "Not completely" my husband replied "He sings all right in the chorus". "I assure you it will be useless, but if you insist we shall lend him a flute and give him a term's lessons which will no doubt convince you". We left for India and when we returned 18 months later it was to hear that Jock was the best flautist the school had produced and was playing in the orchestra.

Some ten years later he spent six months in Labrador in the Grenfell Mission and only recently was I told "He drew music out of a penny whistle that might have come from a flute". Today, in his sixties in a Canadian town he has a weekly gathering of fellow medical men, each with his own instrument, making music together. The moral of this anecdote is that we should never discourage those who so long to find their undiscovered talent.

(*c. 1978*)

# Relationships

## Honour Every Man

These words coming across the radio on the morning service spoke to me of a favourite theme in my mind – the question of equality as against superiority and inferiority. The attitude of our society towards social distinctions has changed immensely in my lifetime. Between aristocracy and the working classes a great gulf was fixed. This was also true between the professions and shopkeeping people. Very markedly it was noticeable between races, and particularly between black and white. People were also separated by their creeds and denominations – Catholic and Protestant, Episcopalian and Presbyterian. Until quite recently we sent missionaries eastward to India, China and Japan to take the Gospel to the peoples of those lands. Nowadays, the stream is reversed and easterners are bringing their ancient wisdoms to our western countries.

'All men are equal in the sight of God' may be accepted on one level but in the sight of man many are handicapped and different, and equality is a difficult conception. The well-worn phrase inferiority complex arouses a response, perhaps, in all of us – 'Yes, I have it'. Inferiority involves being different from others – too rich or too poor, too tall or too short, too fat or too thin. Some children of friends of mine born with titles and living in a castle, were sent to the village school. On one occasion the eldest of them came home bitterly weeping. Asked why she was crying brought the answer, "It's not fair! A girl in my class has no bathroom in her house and we have three bathrooms – it's not fair!" This illustrates vividly how too much as well as too little may cause us to grieve.

Another instance which I remember was of an under-privileged working family who won the pools. They came to me asking for help in their distress. They now had a big house, modern furniture and fine clothes, everything money could buy but, alas, no friends. We can multiply these instances indefinitely, but it is in our own lives that we must seek for understanding. Let us take the symbolism of the high road on which we can travel with others, sometimes, it may be, a bit ahead of them; at others, lagging behind, but still the road is there and we jostle each other as we walk towards our destination.

It is commonplace nowadays to find members of the aristocracy in business, even becoming shopkeepers, and still more common to find the sons and daughters of working-class people becoming professors, judges, hospital chiefs – positions which in the past were reserved for the so-called upper classes. As individuals, such people have to make adjustments which are by no means easy and at times scarcely within their power. They may carry throughout their lives some apologetic awkwardness or, in contrast, some over-bearing condescension, but they find great difficulty in the assurance of equality, the jostling on the high road. It is also difficult to accept our equality with murderers, thieves, and criminals of all sorts. Can we find the answer in the humility which says to the man on his way to the gallows 'There but for the grace of God go I'?

Can we then in truth honour all men? Can we find in ourselves both the virtues and the vices, the pride and the humility, the awareness through understanding that in the sight of God all men *are* equal? It is in this equality that we can find the peace and the joy that make life really liveable.

(*c. 1980*)

# Conception

Quite frequently in the course of my work, patients come to me complaining bitterly about their unwantedness, convinced that their conception was not a matter of love, but in some way fortuitous, and that the mother thought of her pregnancy as a burden and a mistake.

The whole question of psyche/soma, spirit and body, and their relationship, must have interested me very early in my life. I can recollect that in my teens I was aware of differing speculations about this body/soul relationship. One theory I remember was that the quickening of the child in the mother's body indicated that the soul had entered the flesh. Others insisted that this happened at birth, while the third theory which always seemed to me ridiculous, was that at the 5th year, or even the 7th, this communion occurred.

Common sense seems to make it quite plain that the psyche must pre-exist and enter the soma at the time of conception, when the fusion between the parental cells is established. Working as I have done in the psychological field for almost 50 years I have met with many patients who seem aware that their lives have been much influenced by the circumstances of their conception. Many have a great grudge against their parents because this took place out of matrimony.

In the many cases of adoption that have come my way, I realise how, before adoption, there has been inevitable rejection. During the days of pregnancy which must seem very long to the developing child, the influences of the mother's emotions are extremely important. The physical composition of the hormones in her bloodstream vary according to her mood. When a pregnancy is welcomed and a matter of rejoicing, the child is secure, well cared for in her love. If, however, fear, anger and hatred are dominant, the hormones will create a situation of insecurity, anxiety and distress.

It is common nowadays for adoption to take place early in the child's life, although well-meaning counsellors advise delay while searching enquiries are held into all the circumstances of the case. Even, however, a few days after birth, the child in an intimate relationship to the original mother may have a strange but very real awareness either of the suffering caused to the mother by her renunciation of the infant, on her hardness of heart, and relief at getting rid of her burden.

It is possible that both these attitudes are present, and alternate at this time. The infant must certainly be aware of the change in his circumstances. Let us remember how acute is the sense of smell in the new-born, and now that the odour of the milk-secreting breast is gone, loss and bewilderment must develop.

Nowadays, parents are advised to make no secret of adoption, and from the first questionings of the child, they should be open, and disclose the truth. This, however, is no easy matter. The parent may have difficulty owing to feelings of guilt and embarrassment, and the child may be more aware of these reactions than of the truth the mother is seeking to impart.

Even when parents have done their best in this matter, the child may still be puzzled, and find the process of adoption difficult to understand and accept. In many cases there is great anger against the original mother – 'How could she?' In others, the child seems to be aware of the maternal suffering and in deep sympathy with her loss.

These very early feelings are unlikely to remain in consciousness as the child grows, but being repressed, lying deep in the unconscious, they still affect the total personality as it grows to maturity.

Resentment, by which we mean repressed anger, is common in the lives of such children and often vitiates their relationships with others throughout life. Until this is understood, it tends to persist, with a great lack of forgiveness towards the parents, both the real and also the adopting individuals.

In the Tibetan Book of the Dead, where reincarnation is assumed, a child's psyche is depicted as seeking its way among possible parents, and making the choice of the family into which it will be born, by some inner guidance. Looked at in this light, we can transfer the responsibility from the host to the invading individual. The child who has thought of himself as unwelcome may perhaps glimpse the awareness that he is a gate-crasher, so now the responsibility is on his shoulders rather than on those of the parents.

(*1983*)

# Pedestals and Ditches

Betty had been a patient of mine some years earlier. Her condition then was unsatisfactory to herself and others. She was irritable and made other people cross – ill-adjusted, we would say, to living with other people. One of her chief difficulties was that she would suddenly come to the end of her resources and feel completely drained of energy, at which point she would either leave her job or find herself turned out by an impatient employer. Through analysis we had worked out this withdrawal, and now she came to me to report how well she was doing, and how pleased her employers seemed to be with her. She used a strange expression "You know, they will soon have to get a step-ladder to dust me". "Betty", I said, "What funny things you say. Whatever do you mean?" "Oh, I just mean they think I am marvellous, I am up on a pedestal." "Come down quickly", I said, "Don't you know the Chinese proverb "Don't stand on a pedestal: one step may be fatal?"

Just about that time Ivy was coming for treatment and she brought a sad dream. She had been climbing a ladder and when half way up she slipped into a ditch below. The tragic part of this disaster was that she could not climb out without help, so she felt great despair, not seeing any way of escape from her predicament. Pedestals and ditches – too high up in the world, or sunk in despair. Betty's irritability was traced back into her early life where she had a very difficult childhood. The parents lived in the maternal grandmother's house and Betty was at the mercy of three women, – Granny, Mother, and her own elder sister. They approved and disapproved of her in so many ways that she often found herself in what is now known as a 'double bind' where pleasing one means displeasing another, both of whom are in authority. Grandmother was the important figure in her childhood, the parents both went out to work and sister was at school.

We find ourselves in a quandary if we have to sympathise with the different members of this three-generation household. Poor Granny having her home invaded, demands made upon her with which she could not always cope, her property used and misused, very upsetting to her sense of how-things-ought-to-be. Poor daughter, not able to escape from the parental values and ideas, still trying to combine her three offices of daughter, wife, and mother – a difficult if not impossible task. Poor son-in-law, not master in his own house, dominated by all these women with their ideas as to how he ought to live his life; no wonder he had taken to alcohol, and in so doing further complicated the life of the household. Poor big-sister, at first over-mothered and then pushed out by Betty, now escaping to school and returning as little as possible to the complications of home. And Betty? Her chief loyalty and love were to her grandmother who had nursed her in infancy. Granny became blind, suddenly and dramatically, when Betty was eight years old. One of Betty's neurotic episodes under analysis was an attack of hysterical blindness. Granny died two years later, similarly without warning, and Betty had a panic-fear of death. We learned to look out for this identification with the grandmother when symptoms of illness puzzled the doctors attending her. Ultimately after an analysis, not continuous, but spread over many years, she learned that here was no need to fall ill. She was able, I sometimes thought, to *maintain* that pedestal position, so satisfactory was the important work she carried on into her old age.

And Ivy in her ditch? Can we trace some of the factors that had brought her to such despair? She was the youngest member of a big family of boys and girls. The parents had professional status but were poor, and Ivy's conception had been hailed (so it was record- ed) as 'the last straw'. Boys were more valued in the family, so her femininity did nothing to redeem her from unwantedness in her mother's eyes. Her life had been one of *striving* to excel, (notice that in the dream she fell off a ladder), always climbing to greater heights of goodness to win approval, always helpful at whatever cost to herself, denying herself adequate necessities so that the other poor might be fed. She had a stormy analysis since she pro- jected on to me the image of the rejecting parents, and thought of me as quite impossibly endowed with ultimate goodness. Her feel- ings were those of a young, immature child, which we call proto- pathic, all-or-nothing, 'if I can't have a whole loaf I am not going to accept a half'. She threw the baby out with the bathwater, rejected her analysis, and did not, I think, ever satisfactorily emerge from the ditch, a symbol for lack of feeling for herself.

These two cases bring up the question of success or failure in analytical work. Are we under the necessity of putting our patients one day into this category or that? One of my more critical colleagues often accused me of forgetting or repressing awareness of the unsuccessful cases. One of the seven deadly sins in *hubris*, pride, self-satisfaction, and I suppose its opposite is *acidia*, despair, depression, self-abasement. We must guard against these opposite attitudes in our work as analysts. We must see outselves as *agents* in the processes of the developing integration of the personality but must not identify ourselves with the *cause* of the growth. Ambrose Paré on the field of Agincourt said "I dress their wounds, God heals them". As a student in the surgical wards, I remember seeing the stitches drawing the tissue edges together and marvelling at the process of Nature that closed the seam. And so the analyst: standing by, like an obstetrician, marvelling at the emergence of the creative principle; intervening with a minimum intrusion of his own thought, knowing that forces are at work, more than personal in their nature, and so unceasingly keeping faith with these forces and expecting life to triumph over death.

Parents are often very deeply ashamed that their children are recommended to have analytic treatment. It reflects, they suppose, on their capacity to be 'good' parents, and they feel themselves judged and condemned for their so-called failure. My husband and I had four children, and three of them committed themselves early in life to the processes of analysis, to discover the ways in which their own personal life-energy had been allowed to flow, to develop, and to bear fruit; or on the other hand, to learn how parents, teachers and the environment of their childhood had conspired to hinder and sabotage its development and frustrate the full growth of their capacities. I was inevitably discovered to be a 'bad' parent with only patches of goodness. I could comfort myself that I was extremely similar to the parents whom my patients on the analytic couch picked to pieces in their hours with me ('psychoanalysis is an expensive method of picking holes in parents'.) I remembered, as some consolation, that their infancy and childhood lay in the preanalytic period of my life, when there was little or none of the present-day filtering of the teaching derived from analysis available for parents. Nowadays parents have Benjamin Spock and a dozen other 'experts' to advise us but in those days we could not even spell 'psychology'.

In the calmer waters of old age, I can be extremely thankful that my children know me as 'bad' as well as 'good', and , since it is also *their* fate to be so judged, that we have to come into an acceptance of each other which has made them my friends on the basis of equality. This word equality expresses a very blessed state which it may well take a lifetime to achieve. Sadly enough, in many lifetimes we do not attain it fully, but still find ourselves on the seesaw of emotional distress, either teetering on our pedestals of superiority or ditched despairingly in our inferiority. Through analysis, which enables us to accept the sybil's command "know thyself", we learn how very like other folk we are, fellow travellers on the road of life, sometimes jostled, it may be, into the ditch or up on to the ridge above, but if we keep in touch with the others we are ultimately secure enough in their company.

Alfred Adler, the Viennese contemporary of Freud, first brought the words inferiority complex into contemporary language. He pointed out that all human beings begin life with an *actual* inferiority, because as babes they are unable to feed or clothe themselves and are entirely dependent on adults. Life is given them to rid themselves of this inferiority, and early enough in life the child loves to emulate his parents with 'I can do it'. As parents we must say 'yes' to this urge. A Scots saying is 'Can do is easily carried about'. The sabotaging parent says 'you are too small', thus reinforcing the inferiority and postponing the attainment of equality. Whenever possible it is wise and right to encourage the child, helping him to trust his emerging capacities, fostering his brave attempts to do things as grown-ups do them, taking pleasure, genuine pleasure, in his achievements. He will meet discouragement soon enough, and siblings and other jealous rivals will see to it that he won't climb too high.

Inferiority is felt by the individual not only in being too small, too poor, too low-born, deformed or ugly, but strangely enough in the opposites: he is too well-endowed with intelligence, too tall, too wealthy, aristocratic, titled or outstandingly good-looking. It seems as if any attribute that removes him from a sense of equality is a threat to his well-being (superiority also brings alienation). Equality, finding oneself one with the others in the stream of life is never easily attained. Adler stresses the value of compensation in the face of inferiority, or even perhaps the value of *conscious* inferiority in evoking the striving for excellence. Demosthenes with his speech defect became a great orator, Beethoven with his deafness the supreme musician. Adler himself was a very small man, which gave him understanding of one inferior situation and probably motivated his opposition to Freud in Vienna.

Over-compensation, inflated valuing of the self that is not backed by real work, real striving, is destructive. It cannot be maintained, it leads to bad relationships, and is the product of childish fantasy where magic rather than solid endeavour achieves the desired end. In Christ's teaching it is the meek who inherit the earth. Who are the meek? Perhaps they are those who are courageous and determined enough to find the way, whether it is the middle way of the Buddhists, the road to equality of Adler, or the highway of Christ who made himself of no reputation but took on himself the role of servant, who called his disciples friends and taught the way of perfect equality. To inherit the earth is a great reward.

(1979)

"Lord, we know what we are, but know not what we may be."

*Shakespeare*: Hamlet

# What's in a Name?
## Some Thoughts on Relationships

Early Jewish history relates how Moses demanded of the Almighty that he should provide a name. How else could Moses act as intermediary between the Israelites who were his responsibility in the wilderness, and God, to whom he and they owed allegiance?

Have we today the same difficulty? Who listens to us if we talk about God? Isn't God dead? 'All that religious stuff' is so often unacceptable.

We read that Moses was given a somewhat puzzling answer, still difficult for us today – "I am that I am". We may remember, however, that it was not given in English! My orthodox Jewish friend tells me that in Hebrew the verb to be has a beauty and depth of significance that we totally miss in translation. In the German language we get *Ich bin* and *Ich werde*, the former is 'here and now I am' *–ego sum* – but the latter is more, the dynamic something is becoming (happening), something is at work, and who knows what the outcome will be? Perhaps we can write "Who knows", God knows, since God contains past, present and future. All time is eternally present. God's presence is with us till the end of time. "Lo, I am with you always, even to the end" were words spoken by the Logos.

How am I to speak to people today about this God? The High and Holy one? Our Father in heaven. His name shall be called Wonderful, Counsellor, the Mighty God, the Everlasting Father, the Prince of Peace. Will people listen and understand? In the Synoptic Gospels of the New Testament, two names are given for the Christ that will be born: Emmanuel, meaning God with us, and Jesus, meaning Saviour. In St. John's Gospel, Christ is the Logos, the word by which God speaks to man. In St. Paul's writing, the Logos is identified with the Holy Spirit, "Christ *is* that Spirit".

Often folk come to consult me about difficulty and frustration in their lives. For instance, a well-equipped, intellectual man, who fails to get promotion, and consequently suffers from inferiority and depression. He is somewhat condescending in his decision to become my patient as his academic achievements put him in a different category from any scholarship to which I could lay claim. He decided to impose only one condition which he introduced by saying, "When the radio starts talking about God, I switch it off, so I warn you, keep off that subject, or I shall break off the analysis". I promised to try to avoid religious topics and soon we were in the toils of deep analysis dealing with his early years. My unconscious, however, took over one day and I found I was talking to him of "a spirit other than our mortal own", which is how Edward Carpenter has taught us to speak of the divine presence. I apologised and awaited his exit, but no! "You can go on now", he said, "I can take it", and, from then onwards, such a subject was no longer taboo. Similar experience has been often repeated in my practice.

But, we may ask, can anything be taboo in the work of exploring the psyche in depth? Poor Freud got into terrible trouble with his academic colleagues in Vienna when he discovered, through listening to his patients, that small daughters had sexual fantasies and desires involving their fathers. The Viennese doctors were shocked, and rejected his teaching, maintaining the taboo which represses such awareness.

Freud, however, was also guilty of prohibiting entry, in his case, into the world of religion, of spirituality – it was all illusion, he affirmed, and what human beings needed for complete adjustment to life was what he called "full genitality", consciousness of, and acceptance of the role of male and female physical maturity. Spirituality he saw as an unnecessary development, God as a superflous hypothesis. How strange that a Jew, whose race had developed and affirmed awareness of God's presence in man, should suffer from such repression.

Jung came along to open up for us knowledge of the spiritual, now acknowledging the psyche as the spirit, and the word libido, which in Freudian terms had been applied to sexual drive, was now used for creative energy far beyond the physical. The creative energy, in Jung's conception, is unconscious, the unseen, intangible, ultimately unknowable psychic energy. He emphasises in his teaching the dynamic creative flow, comprising man's own capacity to create, to be a channel for that, the evolutionary urge, which is ever seeking to give life and, indeed, life more abundant.

As a medical woman, who has worked for so long in the field of analysis, I can now testify that we are indeed foolish to deny the need for full understanding of sexuality and that, by repressing sex, we often land ourselves in trouble, repressing the other valuable aspects of the libido, as well as sexuality. Look, for instance, at curiosity – the need to know, the urge to discover the secrets of being. The parental prohibition of curiosity by such remarks as, 'It is naughty to ask questions', or 'Don't let me find you reading books like that again', make the child guilty by denying him the right to know, not only about sex, but about much else, since without curiosity it is difficult to acquire knowledge.

Again, anger – a child screams with rage long before he is fully conscious. Later, about three years old, he is often a very angry individual, subject to tantrums and noisy irrational demands. His future life-style may depend largely on how the parents deal with this anger. It has to be acknowledged and some expression of it must be allowed, but control is essential. Holding the child tightly in parental arms at such times gives the necessary feeling of security, and the strength of this holding is reassuring and brings calm.

A sad alternative is for the adult to inflict punishment, or to express disapproval with such words as, 'You can't behave like that' or to make use of the parent's superior physical strength to subdue the child, which is very frustrating for the little one. In this case, although it checks the angry storm, it yet fails to accept what is in great need of expression with the possibility of control. Without expression, repression dams the flow and leads to inevitable loss of energy. Does civilization then make anger unacceptable?

Let us concede that anger has a necessary part to play in our lives, that in early childhood it emerges at first in uncontrolled behaviour, which parents must recognise, and find ways of helping the child through his difficulties. Gradually, the crude, primitive fury abates, maturity develops and the valuable anger comes to serve the child – now growing wise – instead of mastering him. We may liken anger to fire, which, you remember, is a good servant when it warms the house and cooks the food, but a bad master when it takes over, out of control, and destroys our property.

I have diverged, it seems, from the quest to know more about

God into the need to know and understand more about the energy that motivates our lives, taking as examples curiosity and anger, but realising that many urges demand expression and can be used creatively, or destructively; they can master us, become compulsive and self-seeking without recognising the claims and needs of 'the other'. Maturity involves the other, and here it is that we learn from analytic investigation how the ego-centricity, the self-centredness so necessary for the young infant, gradually matures, and the importance of the other in relationship becomes clear. Little girls before the age of seven, or thereabouts, think, and perhaps talk, about themselves as mothers, wishing they had live babies instead of dolls, but often many years pass before they realise the need of a husband, the other. The small boy, too, may take a long time to realise that the penis has more to do with life than serving his own body, that it is an organ of relationship.

During this century, and particularly since the disruptive forces of the two world wars, knowledge about sexual matters has become much more available than in Victorian times. Though knowledge comes, yet wisdom lingers, and, judging by the terrible destruction of the family taking place today, we have to ask whether there is a real maturing of sex occurring, with its awareness and need of the other, or whether self-centredness is all too often maintained well into adult life and, indeed, into old age.

Is awareness of the other only a beginning, and does maturity involve the others, not only the mate now, but the family? Children give reality to mating and greatly enrich the relationship. Growth from son to husband and, in due course, into fatherhood is a creative process in the individual – very beautiful to witness when unspoiled by possessive parents-in-law or other factors retarding maturity.

Infatuation, more particularly, perhaps, love at first sight, may be psychologically understood as a trick of Mother Nature, as the first step in the fulfilment of her aim – the establishment of a family. It involves a breaking up of egocentricity, there are now two in the picture instead of the original one. Psychoanalysts – and cynics – see it as a contra-sexual image nurtured in one's own psyche now projected upon another with a great uprush of feeling. The image may be that of the young mother in the first flush of her parenthood, incredibly adorable, but sadly unlike his mother, the ageing woman of the present day. (When a gentleman seems to prefer blondes, has it something to do with a fair-haired mother or a Scandinavian nanny, I wonder?) A sufficiently mature lover will build upon the projection, with appreciation and loving care developing. When mutual, the situation gives supreme pleasure, when one-sided, it may bring great suffering because of rejected and unreciprocated feeling. When this rejection has its roots in early infantile experience, it can be very bitter and persist long after the 'love-affair' is past.

A consideration of these destructive factors brings us inevitably to demand, even to insist, that there must be a remedy for so much going wrong in young families today. Perhaps, it is to be found in an answer to the question asked as heading to this article, "What's in a name?": God's nature and His Name is Love. Turning our backs on God, we lose our capacity for love, neither loving ourselves nor our neighbour, nor discovering the capacity for loving parenthood. Insist? Yes, let us put what energy we have into the pursuit of more awareness, consciousness, mindfulness of THAT "the Spirit other than our mortal own" whose name is LOVE.

(*1982*)

The angels keep their ancient places; –
Turn but a stone, and start a wing!
'Tis ye, 'tis your estranged faces,
That miss the many-splendoured thing.

From: "In no strange land", *Francis Thompson*

# Experience:
# Happenings between People

What is experience? Something one comes through – 'ex' means out of – something we emerge from, and as in, 'I shall never be the same again since I had that experience'. The Oxford Etymological Dictionary gives a tantalising reference to 'pirate' or 'piracy' – certainly it would be some experience to meet a pirate. The adjectives we can apply to experience seem endless. Here are some of them – common, unique, boring, illuminating, perplexing, reassuring, terrifying, unexpected, anticipated, humiliating, enriching, tragic, joyous, puzzling, enlightening, sad, joyful – it seems as if we can add to the list indefinitely.

There is an individuality about experience – it happens to you, to me; yet we can think of family experience, group experience, national experience and, even, in these days of the global village, of planetary experience. Some of us can claim a great richness, a wealth, of experience. This may be through travel, through education and access to learning, through friendship and the people we have known and, more particularly, through those we have loved. And the poverty-stricken folk? have they stayed at home instead of going out to meet the pirates? Anxiety certainly cripples one's ability to confront what life offers in the way of experience. Some of our friends complain that nothing happens from day to day in their dreary existence. They envy the adventurous who are brave enough to face what is happening which, be it safe or dangerous, enriches their lives so that they emerge in some way different. Such people are willing, I suppose, to experiment with their lives, to observe what comes about when they create, or have created, for themselves a new environment, a change of circumstances, a different milieu. How do they react? (In chemistry, we would watch the test-tube for the reaction when a new blending occurs.) Psychologically, these reactions build up to create the sort of person we are – over-cautious, timid, anxious, fearful, or, on the contrary, devil-may-care, adventurous, brave enough to face what comes, meeting it straight on, not turning our backs in retreat.

The conditioning, by which I mean the laying down of patterns of behaviour in life, is now known to occur in the earliest periods. Even before a child is conscious of his outer surroundings, he must be conscious of the maternal relationship, mediated through their shared bloodstream before birth, and by close contact at first through the touch, the feel, even the smell of the mother's body, which varies according to whether she is living a tranquil, peaceful existence, or is disturbed by fear and anxiety. Emotional contagion is just as real and observable as the infection in measles. One definition of fear is 'an expectation of evil', and it is not difficult to find parents or relatives with gloomy forebodings about what is going to happen. We are strangely at the mercy of what we expect – it comes to us out of the blue. I suppose that we create it by our thinking.

What about that pirate we have talked about, who threatens our craft if we are brave enough or foolhardy enough to set out to sea? Pirates may belong to past years and only threaten us through long forgotten tales of childhood, but there are storms and cyclones on the ocean, and even uncharted reefs. What do we expect? Will one brave, courageous person keep a whole ship's crew alert and confident, meeting danger, if and when it comes, and never losing his energy through foreboding and despair?

The ocean is a big symbol of the life of the unconscious. We simply do not know, are completely ignorant of what we shall encounter, even in one hour's time, much less in life as we meet it from day to day. Igonoramus is a term of disrespect, but each of us is unaware of the future, and it matters a great deal to us and to our fellow travellers whether we greet the unseen with cheer or look to the days ahead expecting the worst.

The Good Book, our Bible, is full of reassurance with which we can build up our hope for the future. Trust in a power not our own controlling and ennobling life, is with us for the taking. And what about auto-suggestion, our inner ability to influence our own lives and, perhaps those of many others? We can acknowledge it as real, and practise sometimes, even laughing at ourselves as we say 'Day by day, in every way, I am getting better and better".

I have many friends whom I have never seen. Recently, a letter came from across the sea asking me a question, which awoke memories of my own married life through which I could share experience with the writer. Curiously enough, our husbands had the same Christian name which, it may be, served to heighten the sense of our lives overlapping. The question to which I responded, but to which I had no direct answer, was whether in married life there is the necessity for shock to reawaken love between husband and wife. I was able to contribute my experience, which included many periods of separation with consequent reunion. In every case, there was the shock of a broken companionship but, with honesty, the recollection came that, although always painful, there could also be relief – the feeling of freedom, that it was good for use both to be on our own again, that the loosening of ties had its own advantages. In retrospect, I feel that the 'shock' of reunion was always immensely pleasurable and brought with it that thrill unknown to the ordinary run of married couples, who seldom moved out of each other's company. There was a sense of renewal, of greater mutual appreciation, gladness, and comfort in being together again, and much else.

Sudden illness or accident to one of the married partners also administers shock, in many cases awakening tenderness and devotion which cement the marriage. When death threatens, and we face inevitable separation, the shock may be profound, awakening our repressed and forgotten emotions, so that again we 'fall in love', become infatuated, making him/her again the centre of our interest and love, thus redeeming us from the subtle intrusion of egocentricity which holds up the flow of creative energy, the libido. And death itself? It is painfully shocking when it seems to sever the relationship, but there can be, contrariwise, a wonderful shock of joy, with the realisation that body-death opens the way for fresh awareness that 'spirit to spirit can meet'.

Shock therapy for the treatment of depressive illness was introduced in Europe and America in the interval between the World Wars and great hope centred on the possibility of cure through this attack upon the psyche. It worked in some cases at least, but in many gave only temporary relief. Perhaps the psychiatrist, the physician, benefited more than the patient, since it seemed to supply him with a means of treatment, sadly lacking in those days before the introduction of tranquillisers and mood-changing pharmacology.

Those of us who have visited Epidauras in Greece, the home of medicine, where an attempt was made to treat illness by psychological methods, may remember the snake-pit. This is still to be seen – an underground enclosure into which the patient was thrown to meet the snakes, to come face to face, I suppose, with the shock of his own fear. Presumably the snakes were harmless, as the technicians assure us is the case in electric shock therapy, but perhaps the arousal of instinctive fear brought with it, in some cases at least, an awakening of psychic instinctual energy, the libido, with its healing power.

We look again at the question asked by my letter-writing friend – are shocks necessary in marriage? My guess is that it greatly depends on the mutual capacity for love in the partners. Maturing is not a question of ageing but, rather, depends on the earliest experiences of the child. Love lies, they say, in the contact of one skin with another. When the life-giving breast allows the infant's mouth and face to merge with it, then love between them finds fulfilment, and a loving individual, the babe, sets out on his journey to maturity. How infinitely sad to realise that deprivation in the early months of his life may bring the disastrous inability to give the *sine qua non* of marriage fulfilment, and may create people with the incapacity to give and take love. Experiments on young monkeys deprived of contact with their mothers, have shown that they do not mature and that they never develop the capacity for mating. Fortunately, man has possibilities denied to the other mammalian creatures to whose stock he belongs. The spirit of man does not age as does his body. Man has more opportunities with love throughout his lifespan. When his spirit contacts another spirit, then the miracle of a new birth may occur. Love, tentative and small, like a mustard seed, has in itself the creative possibility. 'Where love is God is' with the infinite possibilities of life. Always something is happening when a seed falls into good soil.

This essay began with a definition of experience as something happening between people, or between us and the Unknown, which we call God. It referred also to the curious possibility that the word pirate was cognate. As I have said, it must be a great shock to meet a pirate and perhaps the meeting will change the whole future of our lives. May I suggest that we brace ourselves for the journey, the voyage into the ocean, the unconscious, that we trust life implicitly, so that we accept all experience as valuable and know that, by meeting what comes, we shall reach the stronghold at the end of the journey which we call the Self, the true centre of our being.

(*c. 1980*)

# Antecedents of Delinquency

The juvenile delinquent occupies a middle place between the difficult child on the one hand and the psychopath or criminal on the other. He is a product, as such, of our century, and of two world wars. There have, of course, always been youthful criminals, trained in the thieves' kitchens or belonging to families whose heredity invites criminality. Just as the Darwins and Huxleys produce men and women of genius, so there are Smiths, Browns and Robinsons some of whose progeny will probably find themselves in prison. Although hereditary factors still demand attention the present-day focus is much more directed on environment. Not only is this the case, but emphasis is to-day tending to be placed further back in individual history. Since the days of St Ignatius of Loyola recognition of the first seven years as formative has obtained in some circles at least. In our day, first Freud startled the world with his theories of infantile sexuality, and later Adler gave us the idea of the 'homunculus' or prototype man, built up in the first years, carrying the patterns of life and values of potency likely to be repeated throughout adult experience. The work of analytic psychotherapy as now practised seems to force recognition upon its workers that prenatal influences are important, particularly the attitude of the parents to the pregnancy, that birth *is all too likely* to be traumatic to the child, and that the early days, weeks and months of nursing are responsible for much of good or ill that afterwards develops in the life of the individual.

The work of the analytic schools in assessing early factors producing delinquency has been verified and is being studied intensively by Bowlby and his co-workers in the Institute of Human Relationship in London. D. H. Stott, whose investigation and report to the Carnegie Trust of the United Kingdom is a contribution of monumental value to everyone interested in the subject, studied intensively 102 delinquent boys. His analysis of their case-histories goes to show that stealing is 'not just wanting and taking', but that persistent stealing occurs 'without much wanting' and is due to aberrations caused by such factors as parental ill-health or quar-relling, desertion or desertion threats, evacuation, emotional estrangement and other unsatisfactory family conditions.

Allow me to postulate for the purpose of this paper that the delinquent is *a member of society who has failed to make relation-ship with his fellows*. He has not developed his psyche sufficiently to love his neighbour as himself. Dr John Bowlby uses the word 'affectionless' as a category, but we might say 'unloved and unlov-ing'. The deprived child is recognised often as poverty-stricken, lacking nourishment and adequate protection, but the fundamen-tal deprivation is that of affection or parental love. Obviously, this affects all classes of society, but it affects them differently. The less-educated, poorly housed, socially deprived are liable to steal, whereas people in better economic circumstances compensate for their deprivations in other ways.

I remember treating two adolescent girls, both suffering from an acute resentment against the parents. Ada's parents were wealthy, but their social duties led them to neglect Ada, who was brought up by a series of more or less sadistic nurses and governesses. She compensated by buying herself at least a pound of expensive chocolates a day. Biddy, the daughter of divorced parents, was less vociferous in her resentment, but she, poor child, had no spare cash. She stole from cloakroom pockets and was branded a thief and a delinquent. Both of these girls acted compulsively and *sub specie aeternitatis* were equally to be pitied or to be blamed. A little reflection and imagination makes us conscious how near to delin-quency our friends and we ourselves may be.

Social status does not, of course, exclude the individual from the rank of delinquency. The strength of the compulsion may over-whelm the moral sense or the conventional standards of the family. Resentment against the parents may be so strong that the necessity to shame them is a factor. It is also the case that a boy might be expelled from a public school for an act barely considered delin-quent in other societies.

The delinquent is, then essentially developed from the deprived child, egocentric, incapable of loving and accepting love. Not all deprived children, however, become delinquents, but the stigma of their deprivation shows itself in other ways and is widespread in all communities and classes in this country to-day. 'Ada' may grow into a hypochondriac suffering quite real diseases; 'My ulcer' is demonstrable in many ways, and 'My migraines' upset home and office as much as they upset me; but 'Ada' is not delinquent. She carries her self-indulgence through life, and in old age complains bitterly of her lack of friends, blaming circumstances or even a convenient God in the sky. Her acquaintances probably think of her as very brave and wonderfully cheerful in adversity, but because of the initial deprivation she has not the capacity to live fully and know that giving and taking is the law of life. She fails to contribute her quota to the needs of the community, but this is masked by ill-health and fragility of mind and body which is likely to provoke pity rather than blame. 'Biddy', having once been branded as delinquent is likely to become the victim of her 'bad name' and to earn much more blame than pity in the course of her unsatifactory career.

Deprivation is essentially deprivation of love and of the sense of being valued and appreciated. In the artificial life that civilisation has forced upon mankind, parents seem to-day particularly culpable in regard to their offspring. The act of begetting and the awareness of conceiving are all too seldom occasions of absolute bliss and unalloyed rejoicing. To the man it may be an urge to release his tensions, not very different from other satisfactions he has practised all his life, to the woman something she owes the husband as a duty. The resulting offspring, growing for 280 days immured in the womb, may have to suffer grave discontents in the parental milieu. Phylogenically, aeons of time separate the single-celled creature from the human being, so one must realise that ontologically the 280 days are of aeonic importance to the developing child. In these months, even if one were to deny him an immaterial psyche, he is undoubtedly at the mercy of his mother's endocrine balance. If this is emotionally weighted with fear and disgust, as over against love and rejoicing, the infant cannot but be affected adversely. The so-called illegitimate babe was at one period of history thought of as a love-child, and so he still may be accepted and an object of rejoicing. Love children were valued as likely to have special virtues and qualities. Nowadays, unfortunately, they constitute a serious proportion of our delinquent and criminal population, due to their rejection or non-acceptance by their parents in the developing period.

In the teaching of midwifery until recent years the infant was regarded entirely as an object. Pity was expended on maternal suffering, but little or none on the agony of the child. Through analytical work it is now realised that the child suffers both physically and psychologically. The pressure exerted on the head gives rise to severe physical pain. It is not at all unusual on the analytic couch to have a patient re-live the pain and terror of birth, often with subsequent relief from recurrent headaches. Fear of birth seems to be linked with fear of death. Since the infant has no experience to guide him into certainty of life beyond the womb it must seem to him more likely that he will die. He may interpret birth as a rejection and the 'cruel pains' as destructive towards him. Many mothers go into childbirth as if they were going into battle, with a probability of disaster or death. It is here that antenatal care may greatly help mother and child. The mother who knows something of what is happening to her is likely to be less afraid than if she is quite ignorant and uninformed. An easy birth, not unduly prolonged, makes for a good start in the other world for the child.

A difficult birth with much suffering may well affect the child, who can only interpret his suffering as due to maternal hatred and ill-will. Reich says, "All birth is rejection", and analysts agree that it carries great possibilities of trauma. At birth a child may either be received with appreciation, be valued and loved, or he may be 'not wanted', rejected, since he (or she) is not of the desired sex, because he imposes a burden on the parents, or for some other reason. He may be cuddled warmly to the mother's body and allowed to nuzzle at her breast, soon stimulating the flow of milk and satisfying himself at the living stream. On the contrary, he may be 'institutionalised' straight away, have a substitute nipple and substitute milk. In the sensitive state of the new-born, when touch, temperature, smell and tenderness mean everything he either receives and is blessed, or is deprived and suffers grave loss.

The importance of breast feeding lies in its function not only of nourishing the child but in establishing a vital relationship between him and his mother. The mouth and nipple are created the one for the other; the mouth needs the breast and the breast needs the sucking child. A true symbiosis exists of taking and giving between them which is the prototype of relationship throughout life. The infant has his first pleasure in sucking and is satisfied with the milk. The mother has, perhaps, the greatest pleasure of which woman is capable, of being sucked and in the release of her tensions. The twain are indeed one flesh, and at the breast the son is initiated into the meaning of love with its pattern of receiving and giving, the little daughter into an identification with her mother through which she will in time come to her own motherhood. One wise old teacher, William MacDougall, wrote, when occupying a professional chair in the United States: "It is the baby's bottle, not the father's which might well be an object of national prohibition".

Breast feeding keeps the mother near to her child, in touch with him at every four hours; she cannot escape and live a life apart. Bowlby and others now teach that in the first year no mother should leave her child, yet how few observe this necessity. From one unloving generation to another this desire to be free of the infant goes on. Mothers are discharged from maternity hospitals nursing their infants, but return at the end of a few weeks or months with the children weaned. Economic necessity may be given as the reason, but surely we rationalise to cover the lack of love. We live in a barren and sterile age when physical factors are given precedence over spiritual values.

Hospitalisation of children involving separation from parents is being studied at the present day as of importance in the causation of deprivation and insecurity which in a significant proportion of cases are factors in promoting delinquency. Bowlby and his team of workers observe in the child in hospital a rapid and serious withdrawal of feeling. Emotion has become painful and is avoided by the child. Since it is through *feeling* that relationship is made, its repression is a serious affair and is particularly traumatic in early life up till the age of five at least. Admission of mothers along with their children, particularly in serious illness, is now regarded as a possibility in some hospitals, while in others, frequent visiting by the mother, particularly at bedtime, is permitted and advised. Many authorites do not approve of visiting because the children cry when the parents leave them, but crying is a natural expression of feeling and less traumatic to the child than the apathy which may occur if the child feels he is abandoned. Two corollaries of Bowlby's work are important – that operations which can be postponed till the child is six or seven should not be undertaken earlier, and that if the mother cannot visit the child some attempt should be made that *one* nurse relates herself to the child as a mother-substitute. This is certainly of great importance in cases when a child is relegated to institutional life for any length of time.

Inadequate housing has, I suppose, always been a serious cause of delinquency. It can be seen to operate in different ways. In the first place adequate space and privacy is a need of humanity which manifests itself strongly in early adolescence, but which can only meet with denial as society is housed to-day. Many delinquents have never had any room of their own, not a cupboard, not a shelf, not a drawer. In such circumstances the differentiation of *meum* from *tuum* is impossible and may well account for the development of 'pinching', 'snaffling' and picking up unconsidered trifles so common everywhere to-day. Secondly, people living at close quarters tend to become irritable, and the child grows up to think of bad language, hard knocks and blows as normal behaviour. Relationship is thought of as hatred, violence, sadism; certainly not as friendliness, peace and love. Perhaps the most destructive aspect of bad housing, however, is the forcing upon the young child the awareness of parental sexuality for which there is insufficient privacy. Presumably, through the ages children have been witnesses of intercourse, but we may guess that if the act is one of love and reverence the child accepts it and integrates the event into his total experience. If, however, it is sadistic, then, again, there is the degradation of relationship. The awakening of the young child to sexual excitement accompanied by ill-will, and complaining, bitterness sets him to patterns of life which are unwholesome and unprofitable.

When children of opposite sexes share a bed there is liable to be activity of a kind that arouses guilt. When parents sleep with their children fantasies are aroused which seriously hinder normal sexual development. Incest, as Freud has demonstrated so clearly in his early writings, is not necessarily an actuality, but whether it be between mother and son, father and daughter, or between brothers and sisters, its occurrence as fantasy is important in early childhood. The severity of the trauma deepens when indiscriminate sleeping arrangements are forced upon children approaching puberty and in their adolescence. I have found that kind, innocent people serving on housing committees are somehow unaware of these aspects of overcrowding. Perhaps to be conscious of the serious effect it has on the lives of many would arouse society to really great effort to put housing in the forefront of national effort.

Associated with poor housing conditions we must note that children reared in cities have the grave disadvantage of lack of contact with mother-earth, lack of exposure of their bodies to light and of their lungs to open air free from dust, petrol fumes and other contaminations. Stunted, unhealthy bodies are unlikely to be associated with sane, integrated minds. Space for their play and some material for adventure are necessities for developing in children initiative and purposefulness. When society deprives them of so much that Nature provides for country-born children, then society must pay and not protest too loudly at the harm delinquents inflict on it when they turn in protest.

The absence of the father through death, war service, or even through the necessities of commercial travelling or such like, operates in more ways then one. It may upset the mother and make her too closely tied up with her offspring. Acting as 'father and mother both,' she fulfils neither function well. The father's absence is of necessity resented by his offspring, since it is a matter of inferiority to lack a parent. His return, however, is likely to be still more deeply resented, and a state of enmity developing between father and son is often the basis of a later enmity between the lad and the authority of the State. A step-father coming in to remedy the deficiency needs to be extremely good-hearted and tactful if he is not to develop similarly a bad relationship leading to the rebellious and recalcitrant lad.

Enough has been said, I think, to make it clear that the delinquent is a problem child whose problems have been allowed to mature and develop. Similarly, a criminal is a delinquent whose difficulties have met with no resolution. The *prevention* of delinquency is an urgent matter, since the *treatment* is very costly, fraught with difficulty, and there is no certainty of success. Prevention must lie in hope of developing better parenthood, which is a task that should lie with great weight on the minds and hearts of all responsible people. Parents are of necessity young and immature, and society must come to their aid. Possibly in schools more can be done in the adolescent years to develop a sense of responsibility. Marriage guidance councils may, perhaps, develop ways of preparing young folk for marriage. I would suggest that in all child guidance clinics, where the young problem child is brought, a great effort should be made actually to *treat* the parents by psychotherapy if they are willing to be helped. Groups of parents can very profitably be helped in this way. Lecture courses for parents run by psychologically trained personnel can do something. The need is for something to be done on a big scale, but wherever an individual is brought into greater responsibility and wisdom, especially if the individual is a parent, some leaven has been put in the meal, and ultimately we may trust the whole will be leavened.

Beyond this, and integral to our hope for the future, is the necessity for town and country planning to be in the hands of men and women of vision and good-heartedness. Their pity for their fellow men and sincere desire for equality of opportunity will provide space, comfort and decency for the growth of the individual. In some such ways the wounds of society will be healed, and an age dawn free from the blight of the children in difficulty whose sorrows affect all civilisation.

(*The Medical Press*, 1952 & *The Bulletin*, 1953)

"No man is an island" *John Donne*

# Intrusion

When, in repeating the Lord's Prayer, we say 'Forgive us our trespasses' I wonder what image this brings into our minds. Do we substitute the word 'sins' or even 'debts'? As a child I lived on a farm surrounded by woods through which we could find the most marvellous paths and discover flowers and ferns otherwise unkown to us. But at every entry we were confronted with a notice 'Trespassers will be prosecuted'. The grownups encouraged us to pay little attention but to be careful to do no damage, since legally this alone could lead to prosecution. Later we made friends with the keeper who would stop and speak to us. These marvellous woodlands still feature in the dreams of my old age. Later in life trespassing came to have not only a physical but also a psychological meaning. We have to ask ourselves 'Into whose life, into whose territory do I trespass?'

We question too about the people who trespass into our lives who are unwelcome in our territory. A few years ago Robert Ardrey wrote an interesting book called *The Territorial Imperative* in which he showed clearly how the birds, the beasts and man all mark out their territory, their stamping ground, inviting into it the ones they want and defending it against others – the intruders, the trespassers. It is perhaps easier to recognise 'those that trespass against us' than to see ourselves in that role. To be interrupted when we have settled down to a task is irritating and may provoke us to anger – a positive use of this inborn defence mechanism. Lovers obviously dislike the intrusion of a third party into their precious intimacy *a deux*. What about the parents when a pregnancy alerts them to the awareness that an intruder is making himself known and will shortly be making demands as he enters their territory – the family life? Some children surely enough are wanted and warmly welcomed into the family but others are unwanted and perhaps greeted by warning signs against trespassers and gatecrashers. Each babe is said to bring his own quota of love with him as he enters the world; but an initial rejection of the pregnancy may leave its mark on the personality, so that he goes through life expecting that he is unwanted, always expecting rejection.

I feel sure from my experience with the treatment of anxious, insecure people, that this need to be wanted conditions human life with great intensity. Initial rejection is not easily compensated. Many difficult children growing up into unhappy adult life carry this stigma of unwantedness. Many, if not all, illegitimates carry this sad stamp upon their lives, however tender adoptive parents may be. Nature protects the young bird or animal against rejection. Instinct leads the bird to build a nest to receive the products of conception and give them a nested home. What have we lost in developing our human nature? Seeking to answer this, can we ensure that the security of the family is of prime importance for each individual and set ourselves to educate the young before marriage and in early married life to consider the need of their offspring for this security, the affirmation of wantedness in their lives?

Recently a man in his thirties entering a dream group for the first time reported to me with obvious surprise and pleasure that the other members had welcomed him into their fellowship. Can we take notice and make it a habit to welcome newcomers into our territory? The new boy at school, a new girl in the well-established community, need the welcoming voice and gesture. Our generosity in such situations may, for all we know, give a new warmth to the life of the stranger.

In many parent-child situations there is great need of mutal forgiveness. Parents who reject a pregnancy often over-compensate by a possessiveness of the unwanted child, which is so easily mistaken for love. There is hope that, through analytical treatment bringing insight, forgiveness may come. How often do we need to reiterate 'Tout comprendre c'est tout pardonner' – to understand all is to forgive all? Parental arrogance and superiority, which make parents sure that their way is the only right way, hinder their child's initiative and his courage. If they can be humble and speed the development of new ideas and new ways of doing things in the next generation, they may well be rewarded by seeing their children as pioneers, discovering fresh openings on the road of life.

"As we forgive those that trespass against us" – the intruders. Are we still meeting them in our lives and how can we deal with them? To what extent can we tolerate them? Perhaps we may remind ourselves of the permission to enter the woodland, 'provided you do no harm'. Our lives, our territory, our 'woodland' may sometimes have to put up warning notices. With a family of growing children, each of them needing attention and comprehending love, it may well be wise for parents to see themselves as needing protection from outside interests, and that it is unwise to let outsiders or outside interests intrude at that time. Highly trained professional women are caught up in conflict at such times in their lives and have to make important decisions. Perhaps it may even seem that there is a choice as to whether to consider the clients, or patients, as outsiders so that their own children as insiders can feel they are wanted. As the years pass the situation changes and for the mother to resume her profession may give the children the freedom they need in adolescence.

Can we recognize ourselves in the guise of intruders, trespassing unwanted into territory that seems so desirable to us? 'The grass is greener on the other side of the fence.' Do we need to obey the 'Keep Out' notices? Do we need to realise that every one has a right to a life of his own, a right to put up fences as long as there are gates through which others may enter? High stone walls protecting our territory, keep out those who would befriend us, would bring gifts into our lives, would fertilise what grows in our woodland. Can we let them enter or must we be ever on the defensive in case they might do us harm? Frequently those walls are built up in early childhood by over-protective parents. Some of them fear the break-down of class distinctions which today, we see, can be destroyed to great advantage. They may fear 'germs', the infection of unwelcome ideas or, later, dread mésalliance if foreigners are allowed to enter the house. Too much protection and the stock becomes incestuous and fails. Fresh blood gives vitality and greatly increases the possiblity of new gifts, as the genes are gathered from a wider field.

I like to quote lines from an old Scots poet, William Dunbar, author of "The Three Estates". He wrote:

> Ah, freedom is a noble thing
> Freedom makes man to have liking.

Each of us who values freedom in his or her own life moves into a region where freedom for others can be the accepted way. Evolution occurs as each generation takes opportunities for further progress and growth. The protection of new life is necessary – seedlings must not be trampled underfoot – but let us build light fences which can be surmounted, rather than heavy stone walls which imprison. Perhaps if trespassing can be forgiven according to our petitions, we can then expect another upward movement in the race of mankind.                    *(1979)*

# The Need to Know

Once upon a time – was it you? I know for certain it was I, Winifred, who desperately *wanted to know*. The grown-ups were not very helpful since they had forgotten how very very painful it could be to have so much not-knowingness in their lives. The six honest serving men of whom Kipling wrote so wisely – How? Why? When? What? Where? and Who? had become old and tired, the questions were no longer strong and insistent, battering at closed doors. Instead they had given up the hope of getting the doors to open and had gone asleep outside. The flame of 'I need to know' had flickered and died out for want of the supply of energy that earlier had been so urgent, so strong, in its need.

We encounter many dull children and if it interests us sufficiently for us to ask 'Why this apathy, this lack of interest and contentment with ignorance' the answer might well be that no one had listened to their questions and consequently, inevitably, they had abandoned hope of finding answers, and become content to accept ignorance, the not-knowing, thus accounting for the dullness that afflicted them so painfully. Paradoxically we acknowledge that the psyche is also the victim of a need to not-know. In relationship with Cosmos or even with the accumulated wisdom and knowledge acquired through the ages, how puny the intellect of any average ordinary human being! Agnosticism, in its original sense, implies not-knowing, a state that must be accepted and tolerated. Humanity is like that; we are all in the same boat each of us nevertheless as individuals finding his/her own ego-situation between the great libidinous urges, creative when we co-operate but destructive when denied unacknowledged.

This condition was beautifully illustrated in a dream contributed to a group. The dreamer, a woman in her third decade, sees herself in a crowded boat, crowded with people like herself. (Men in uniform were around and also fierce dogs on leash snarling and dangerous) Her interest and attention were focussed on a small boy not yet school age, very lively, full of adventurous spirit who had no sense of fear, but was climbing the gunwale of the boat, in danger of falling overboard. She was terrified on his behalf on three counts – firstly his own lack of fear which she felt would land him in the water and lose his life through drowning. Secondly the dogs might break their restraining chains and the wolf in their nature set upon and devour the child. Thirdly the fear of the uniformed men whose duty it seemed to imprison them. The dreamer awoke in great distress and anxiety fearing for the survival of the beautiful four year old boy.

It was a short term group and only a quick, perhaps superficial interpretation seemed to be feasible. The four year old boy, not yet at school, represents the contra-sexual creative unconscious, the archetype Jung has taught us to call the animus. The dream represents her fear of its repression (the drowning) or of its imprisonment through the super-ego demands with others all in the same boat, civilisation and imprisoning force – or of its destruction by the untamed instinctive murderous instinct if not held in leash. Clearly the dreamstate danger threatens her life now, the dream deals with here and now, in relationship with the four year old pre-school child. It is egocentric, depicts the dreamer's problems still unresolved, but urgent. There is also the grim reminder that our world is full of people like ourselves, the problem not only individual but also affecting humanity imprisoned in the mores of civilisation. Probably the dreamer's sexuality rather than her curiosity was the focus of this picture; but curiosity, sex, anger, fear are all linked closely in the unconscious along with the other elements of the creative libido.

If repression of curiosity gives rise to dullness we may also see that repressed fear causes anxiety, repressed anger, a supine weakness of purpose and self-assertion, repressed sexuality to impotence, frigidity and lack of creativity. The repressed instinct cannot be sublimated, so that there is loss on many levels of the birthright of creative energy. Perhaps we may notice particularly the vitality of the pre-school child, not yet under the domination of civilised society, and ask where and how we can take action to conserve this energy, so badly needed throughout life.

Recently I strayed 'by chance' (I always use these words ironically) into a gathering of educationalists. We listened to a lecturer who argued for the demolition of our existing educational system. Education, he averred, might with advantage cease when the child had learned reading, writing and arithmetic at the primary school.

He gave no suggestion as to what was to happen next, in what paths were the teenagers growing intelligence to be guided, for marriage or its modern equivalent nowadays occurs in the later teens. I was prompted to break into the discussion making two points. The first was that teachers take on the child at the age of four or five *after* the patterns of life have been set. Prenatal life and the first year after birth are of enormous importance in determining the future course of life. The parental attitude to the pregnancy affects the developing child in a way to which greater attention needs to be directed. A rejected pregnancy with, it may be, attempted or desired abortion, followed by rejection at birth, 'We never wanted this brat' or even, sadly common, 'We are so disappointed, we hoped it would be a boy/girl'. The parent is unwilling to accept, unwilling to recognize how their own self-will strongly influences the child's development. So it is clear that the teacher is entrusted with a human being already set on one life-road or another, one of security and wantedness giving him a sense of his own world, or on one of unwantedness, a path of much greater difficulty to travel. I then asked the gathering at what point education for parenthood was to start and what form it was to take. There was no answer and my thoughts drifted back to the earlier and yet earlier stages in life of the young immature parent. My curiosity, *my need to know*, found the satisfactory clue as to how and when parental education begins.

I have quoted the statement 'The repressed instinct cannot be sublimated' by which I mean the psychic energy which the instinct carries, in this case the instinct of curiosity, becomes unconscious, frozen; we have become unaware of its existence and so it is not available in our lives. Puzzling over the meaning of sublimation when first I entered the field of psychological knowledge, I attended a lecture by Alfred Adler, the Viennese contemporary of Freud. His statement shed great light on the process as he stated "We cannot sublimate into thin air. We must sublimate in the presence of our neighbour". I have always been grateful to Adler for shedding that light on the process. It takes up with take-hold-give where the giving is essential to the vitality of our energy – and we say that the Dead Sea is dead because it takes and holds and doesn't give again. It has no outlet.

Our closest neighbours on the tree of Life in the evolutionary process share with us most of the instinctive drives, but use them directly on the plane for the immediate purpose, with the exception of the parent. The animal eats if it is hungry, but in the mothering period she denies her own hunger to feed her young. Is it possible that this instinct then evolves in the course of the ages into the kindness (kinship) of man for his neighbours? Are animals protected against the debasing of their instinct by their lack of choice? Humanity in its evolution has learned how to make decisions and choice has developed areas of the forebrain to serve this purpose. Each individual has some infinitismal share in influencing the evolution of the race. So let us see to it that we choose to act as Adler suggested with our neighbour's well-being in our hearts, not only our own. "Thou shalt love thy neighbour as thyself". The truths and the wisdom that we call psychological were written long ago, curiously enough can be used lovingly to elucidate our neighbour's problems and difficulties to help him when he fails to understand. Let us however be warned against cruel probing, 'trespassing' into territory where our solicitude is resented as unwelcome.

(c. 1980)

I fled Him, sown the nights and down the days;
I fled Him, down the arches of the years;
I fled Him, down the labyrinthine ways
Of my own mind; and inthe mist of tears
I hid from Him, and under running laughter.

"The Hound of Heaven" *Francis Thompson*

# Old Age

## Understanding Our Ageing Parents

Old parents were once young parents. Life has a little joke express-ed in the French proverb 'Si jeunesse savait, si vieillesse pouvait', which we translate 'If youth but knew, if age had but the power'. It is, of course, a tragedy rather than a joke; 'If only' makes so little sense. Young parents are of necessity immature, they are still lear-ning about life. Landed with babies, what do they know? Precious little? Everything?

I think this depends to a very great extent on whether they have belonged to a family in which the heart rather than the head has been the governing factor. Let us consider three different kinds of women who will ultimately become grandmothers. At the moment they are young things.

There is Mrs. A. She has been a student, perhaps an educa-tionalist or a doctor, a research worker or even an archaeologist! She has now married and is expecting her first child. She goes to the library and chooses books on child nurture. She needs to know from *books* because she has lost contact with her own feeling. All mothers, of course, read books and magazines and it is good that they should do so, but the girl I am talking about depends too rigidly on what other people say. She has sacrificed her feeling to her book-learning. She is anxious, very careful, she distrusts nature and has no spontaneous joy in her child. She decides beforehand *not* to feed at the breast, but depends on a bottle and 'Formula', an American term for humanized milk. When the child grows up she often says "I did everything the book said, how strange that he/she doesn't appreciate what a good parent I am." Because of her lack of feeling it is probable that the relationship with her husband is also one of the sharing of thought and opinion rather than of affection. In this family it will be difficult for love to develop.

Mrs. B. is an ordinary girl brought up in school and on the street, neither very brainy nor stupid. Her education has been much the same as her brothers' with no emphasis on home-making, no preparation for motherhood. She thinks of marriage as giving her a better status in her world, and she likes having a man around, as without him she is unsure of herself. She wants 'a good time' and if she becomes pregnant either before or soon after marriage, the child may be thought of as an intruder, not really wanted, a bit of a pity. Later in pregnancy she becomes reconciled to the idea and when the child is born 'He brings his own love with him'. This is probable if she suckles him at the breast and devotes herself to him for the early part of his life. If, however, he is put on the bottle, left in a day nursery or otherwise disposed of while she returns to work, the child knows his rejection, no relationship is established and he is condemned to being 'hard-hearted', perhaps for the rest of his life.

Mrs. C, the third woman, is a good-hearted girl, warm loving, not necessarily good at books, but essentially motherly. She *wants* her baby, knits and sews his garments and looks forward to feeding him at the breast. When he emerges into the world at birth this babe is born into a spiritual womb, welcomed, held in her arms, shared with the husband so that he, in turn, develops his fathering capacity. The 'ferment' in this family is love, and it is this which promotes the growth to maturity. We can take the analogy of yeast – it doesn't multiply or ferment in the cold, it needs warmth, to be kept near the fire, so that the leaven grows and can leaven the loaf. Breast feeding, intimate loving relationship with the father, and beyond that with the neighbours and other people, make the home a warm place in which the natural growth of love takes place. This heritage is likely to establish the lives of the children as happy people and we recognise clearly nowadays that happy children are likely to develop into the right sort of grown-ups.

The first mother, Mrs. A, the university graduate, is now an old lady, her husband has died. She is a grandmother and the proposal is made that she should live with her daughter and her husband. I would like you to envisage what is likely to happen. The old lady is a perfectionist and very opinionated, and because of her rigid patterns the daughter has resentment against her and the older woman's 'helpfulness' in keeping things straight creates tension. This, because it affects the daughter, who after all has the right to be mistress in her own home, affects also every member of the household. Even when Grannie comes for short visits the family tends to get keyed up and the children behave increasingly badly because of the strain. Permanent residence can be disastrous since irritation and bad temper make such a bad background for children's lives.

Since Mrs B. was not an adequate mother she missed the opportunity of growing into an old age marked by wisdom and maturity. As a grandmother she is unlikely to provide love and understanding to the young family. In my experience such women are often very possessive, as if trying to compensate for the early days when they opted out of the experience of holding their infants with the warm embrace they needed. Because of this possessiveness they are apt to interfere with members of the household. They are self-centred and claim from the daughter attention and service that is really due to the husband and children.

The third case where a really loving relationship has been established has much better possibilities of success. Even here there is need of space, both actual room in the house to which the older people can withdraw, and inner space, by which I mean that the older people should live to great extent their own lives with their own interests. Such people are more willing to serve than to be served, and also more willing to understand than needing to be understood and flattered.

Grandfathers fall into similar categories. Some have rigid habits of thought and are full of criticism and disapproval which do not make for a relaxed atmosphere. Others are lacking in human warmth and understanding. But we can be thankful that there are those who will always lend attentive ears to their children's and grandchildren's troubles and help them to see ways of understanding and forgiveness.

We may continue by considering the situation of middle-aged 'children' in relationship to ageing or aged parents, perhaps in their second childhood. It must be conceded that the conditions are far from easy. Even loving, tolerant, easy-going people, in their fifties and later, will find the older generation a burden. They may bear it willingly and graciously, but nevertheless it creates a strain and tension better acknowledged and, if possible, understood. We are dealing with a 'reversal of the generations'. Authority, decisive action, planning, providing, approving, disapproving, have changed hands. 'The Children' are now probably owners of the house. They have the management of affairs, the responsibility of earning and spending the main part of the income, the arrangement of suitable times and seasons, the acceptance or non-acceptance of visitors. In many ways, the older people are bound to feel frustrated at no longer having the direction of affairs and annoyed that *their* opinions are not the guiding principles of the establishment.

When the house belongs to 'the children' and the parents have been taken in as guests, the situation is probably less difficult than if the younger folk move in to the parents' house. In the latter case the dominating attitude of the older people may be much more difficult to overcome. Adaptation is likely to involve conflict, 'Whose house is this?', and the older generation's ideas about a thousand and one arrangements may well create tension and difficulty. This will be particularly noticeable when a third generation – one or more grandchildren – are also at home. Teenagers or early twenties have very different ideas of what is amusing, what is respectable, or entertaining, than the grandparents. The middle generation has its sympathies divided, and great tolerance is needed to preserve a peaceful atmosphere.

To understand ageing parents it is, I think, necessary that 'the children' face up squarely to the fact of resentment and the very real need to forgive their parents. This may seem a hard thing to say, but let us be quite sure in our own minds that parents do need forgiveness and that as long as we harbour resentments and are unforgiving, there can be no real peace in the home. If we face the difficulties, acknowledging the realities, then it is possible that solutions may be found. So many of life's problems are undoubtedly a repetition of the frustrations and difficulties we met first of all in our nursery years. The Americans say 'childish behaviour patterns tend to persist throughout life'.

It is sadly and unfortunately true that parents commonly fail in maintaining attitudes of consideration, understanding and love towards their young children. They think it is quite in order to shout or scream in irritation. I believe there are few households where the child escapes being treated with extreme rudeness by his parents in early life. Between adults, in a relationship of employer and employed, for instance, the boss is not likely to bellow at his workers, still less to hit out at them, or he would find himself deserted by his labour-force. Women learn to be very polite to their 'daily workers' or they quickly give notice or just don't turn up any longer. Listen to how parents talk to their children. I quote from a letter written this week. "My husband makes meal-times miserable for us. He glowers at John, criticizes every action, calls him a pig or a disgusting object". Do you know what John feels about his father? I do. He has two feelings, 1. "I ought to love and honour my father", 2. "I hate my father. I wish he would go away and leave my mother and me alone".

John is only a little boy just now, but both these feelings will persist in him throughout life, although he may well forget or repress much of his resentment as he grows older. This, unfortunately, does not mean that he will feel good towards his father, or really loving towards him and, if in adult life they have to live under the same roof, there will undoubtedly be ill-feeling and strife between them. I think John's case is perhaps an extreme one, but many fathers are tyrants towards their children and, from day to day, year to year, they interfere with the things children so love to do with the natural flow of their wants and wishes.

Daughters, similarly, are not always appreciated by their mothers, particularly if 'Dad' makes too much fuss of them. When parents are not warmly and closely bound together in their married life, the stage is set for difficult relationships. A girl of sixteen told me that 'out of the blue' her mother had announced that she could no longer share the father's love; one or other of them must get out. Unusual? Yes, in this extreme form it is unusual, but I quote these cases because I believe that lurking under apparently friendly roof trees these resentments are not uncommonly found.

Let us consider shortly what every family must accept during the growing up period in the home. Parents inevitably discipline their children, either wisely and lovingly or with impatience and anger. But in every case I suppose the parent maintains attitudes towards the family that may be called 'the approval-disapproval situation'. Through this the complacent child identifes with the parent's approval and avoids his displeasure. Others, however, rebel and are always in trouble and under a cloud.

In the teenages, disapproval is apt to become dominant – disapproval of things that are so different in the new generation from 'when we were young'. Clothes, not only their fashions, but also the expense they entail. All this question of how money is spent may be greatly disapproved. Traditions of thrift have been left far behind. Entertainment, late nights, the sort of friends they make, boy friends, girl friends, are all fair subjects of disapproval.

Then marriage and the advent of In-laws: How painfully the stage is often set, and all too often no resolution of the conflict is found.

Fortunately, in the later stage which we are now discussing, the old people are likely to be less determined to have their own way, in fact, they may well be suffering from painful feelings of inferiority, the inferiority of old age. While in their youth they might have been quite convinced of the rightness of their own opinions and methods, 'only one right way of doing things, my way', now they are quite possibly panic-stricken about their lack of decision and 'know-how'.

An unmarried daughter in her sixties living with her mother, is perhaps particularly to be held in our respect, as the situation is so difficult. Consciously or unconsciously, she probably blames her parents for the fact that she has no husband. In some cases, truly enough, they may have interfered in early love affairs, disapproving of her suitors. Scolding is all too apt to develop as the authority and capability passes from one to the other, but fortunately, things do often take a turn for the better when the older parent weakens and really does become a child again. The latent maternal feeling that has been denied in the daughter almost surprisingly shows itself in tenderness and gentle care of the old person and a situation of contentment develops between them.

Understanding is a very precious thing; to understand all is to forgive all, and when we forgive we are healed in mind and in body.

*(In its original form, part of this appeared as "The Reversal of Relationships" in a National Marriage Guidance Council pamphlet in 1962)*

# Why be tired?

Many years ago, Leslie Weatherhead warned that the assumption that everyone must suffer from fatigue was unnecessary. Through an article entitled, "Why be tired?", he was the first, I believe, in this country to write combining depth psychology – that is, awareness of the unconscious – with religious teaching. The story is that, after writing this article, he succumbed to a nervous breakdown.

Do you remember the story of the exhausted husband who, on his half-day off work, is asked by his wife to mow the lawn? A friend suggests a round of golf. They play eighteen holes without any difficulty. 'I want' is the word attaching to the instinctual libidinous energy, deriving from the unknown source on which life depends. 'You ought', or even 'I ought', depend on a fluctuating supply, easily arousing 'But I don't want' with inertia and fatigue.

Recently, on radio, I listened to what seemed an extraordinary statement about women as mothers, indicating that, for years on end, they could not escape from a condition of chronic fatigue, since demands were made upon their available energy by family commitments day and night. The speaker was, I presume unconsciously, depicting cases of neurotic anxiety as if they were woman's normal heritage in motherhood.

I am glad to bear witness to a completely opposite state of affairs in which the whole experience, including matrimony, pregnancy, birth and rearing children, brings joy and energy to bear on the woman's life. Surely this is what Mother Nature intends – a thankful acceptance of the experience – not merely resignation, surely not resentment and frustration, when fulfilling life's demands.

Let us recall, or imagine, the pleasure of swimming in a river flowing with a strong current. Plunging in, we do wisely if we swim against the flow, while we realise how good it is to be immersed and refreshed by the water. It may be hard work with not much progress as we battle upstream. Then a turning point, and we are carried with a minimum of exertion back to our landing place. So it must be in life. No one escapes, but the stimulus we get from plunging into life's difficulties strengthens and enobles our being. Robert Browning has written of this way of life.

> One who never turned his back but marched breast forward,
> Never doubted clouds would break,
> Never dreamed, though right were worsted, wrong would
>     triumph,
> Held we fall to rise, are baffled to fight better,
> Sleep to wake.

Yes, and die in order that we may rise into new life.

Depth psychology teaches us that in the plasticity of life's beginnings we are conditioned, by which we mean exposed, laid open, with vulnerability to life's influences at its maximum. It asks us to admit that childhood's behaviour patterns tend to persist throughout life. Let us listen, then, to some of the admonitions used by parents, particularly by anxious mothers, such as: 'You will tire yourself out.' 'That work is very tiring.' 'Don't get over-tired.' 'You will be tired tomorrow.' 'Don't walk too far.' 'It is important to have a midday sleep'.

Later in life, these grown-up children, because of their early conditioning, can be found stating, 'I am one of those people who require ten hours' sleep.' Even eight hours' sleep nightly consumes one third of our available time for work and play. Is all that sleep necessary, or is an anxious mother still admonishing us? Although she may have died long since, the neurotic care she lavished on her family still hinders their activity.

Scientists, who make a study of adult sleep patterns, have apparently concluded that five hours' slumber is adequate for ordinary people, and that in times of stress they can make do with less. More is a luxury, perhaps enabling us to repress the unacceptable aspects of our day. 'Forget all about it', we seem to be saying, but repression does not rid us of the things that disturb our life – held in the unconscious, they keep their ability to upset our equanimity and give us bad dreams.

Consciousness is to be prized, hard won for the human race as it has evolved. 'Only man knows that he knows', so let us value the awakening.

The Buddhists, teaching us to be mindful of our breathing, are helping us to move towards greater consciousness. Gurdjieff

reiterates the teaching that mankind is asleep and must be awakened. Which of us is going to take on the function of the alarm clock?

The heart sets a good example of continuous work not leading
to fatigue. Each beat, the systole, is followed by relaxation, the
diastole, this rhythm recurring as a rule between 60 and 80 times
a minute throughout a lifetime. Nature sets great store by rhythm,
and we do well to observe and attend to her guidance. Spells of
tension may be followed by awareness that we are due a holiday,
a day of strenuous physical labour and we are glad to rest, not denying the need, yet assured by the return of the energy we need for
the work of the morrow.

For some sturdy people, a holiday is a privilege rather than a
necessity. We even hear them groan over the boredom of having
nothing to do. A change of occupation suits such folk better than
a remission from work. Probably we notice and acknowledge this
as age creeps upon us. We need not lose sympathy with the young
in body, or in spirit, who still demand time and space for the exploration of what awaits discovery in their life experience.

Looking again at the warnings against over-exertion imposed in
childhood by the grown-up wiseacres, let us see how subtly they
become part of our own feeling. 'I must not over-exert myself, or
I shall pay for this tomorrow,' we say, when the extra hour's work
has been undertaken.

'Why be tired?' imposes another question. Does your home (take
it as a symbol of life) run on a battery system and depend on a
private accumulator for the heat, light and power it needs for
smooth running? Or can it remain plugged in to the main supply
so that there is little likelihood of the current failing? Every need
can now be met, the current is available by day and by night – but
we must plug in, the contact with the source must be established
and maintained. No longer is there any need to check the batteries,
no longer anxiety as to what is available – it is all there for us.

So again, the question, why be tired? It is all there but, unless we
are plugged in, the light will fail and the radiators will give no
warmth. How then do we plug in?

I have spent over fifty years of my life working in the field of
psychoanalysis, encouraging and training others to do this work.
I have come to rely on the resources that lie untapped in so many
lives, the unexploited resources and unused potential of the unconscious life, which await discovery beneath and beyond our own

personal consciousness. Literally, it is unknown, although from it springs our life energy – 'it makes us tick'. We can, even through a lifetime, have little awareness of our breathing, of our heart beat, of our digestion, and other autonomic bodily processes, yet how faithfully they serve us.

Dreams emanate from this area of the unconscious as we sleep, and by taking heed of what they tell us, we acquire wisdom valuable to ourselves and to others. An interpreter is needed, but the Buddha told us, "When the pupil is ready, the Master appears," so let us postulate that the interpreter of our dreams will be available when we are ready to meet him.

The question, 'Why be tired?' poses a challenge demanding some awareness of the source of life's energy. Inexorably, we admit 'I am psyche-soma', 'I am soul and body', 'I am spirit and physique'. Not so long ago, philosophers speculated as to when, at what period of life, the soul attached itself to the body. I remember clearly reading in responsible literature that it might be at the age of five! More commonly, perhaps, the guess was at birth or at conception. We may now, I feel, accept the idea that the spirit creates the body, is inherent in every cell of its tissue, and withdraws at, or about, the time of physical death. The tangible, visible body tends to usurp attention and the notion 'I am body, I have a soul' is slow to give way to 'I am spirit, I happen to have a body,' which truth, once we grasp it, enables us to live without the fear of a death in which we are apparently annihilated. So again, why be tired?

Consent we must to the factual evidence that the body has its origin in the zygote, where sperm from the man enters the ovum of the woman, two cells fusing into one, from which a new life begins its existence. In the woman's body this takes on distinctive human form, and entering the outer world develops through infancy, childhood and adolescence, into the maturity of adult life. Reaching the prime of physical life, a peak of strength, of bodily and mental activity, is attained, after which the inevitable downhill journey is faced, until the gate of death opens and we leave the body to disintegrate.

So again, the question, 'Why be tired?' demands an answer. The body is wearing out, no longer fit for strenuous exertion, a mile's walk now seems too far, lifting a heavy weight impossible. Memory, too, is playing tricks on us, it seems that the brain fails to register things as it did in our heyday. Frailty of body and mind must be faced and accepted, not without a desire to claim endurance. Bodily needs become simplified in old age, but require some attention – simple adequate diet, maintenance of the body heat, sleep, giving time and heed to dreaming, an open window, a measure of aloneness, since a crowd becomes tiresome, although human contact remains desirable. Radio and television brings stimulus and company when needed and – greatest blessing of all – they can be switched off.

The energy of the spirit need not decline with physical frailty, although sadly, it so often does, and we find old people retreating into the self-centredness of infancy, claiming attention, demanding service, and surrendering their ability to walk on their life's journey without crutches. By and large, the prescription for a happy and useful old age is to make use of our resources, and now I am asking you to look with me at the aspect of life which is more than physical. I would ask you to envisage an underlying area of life, hidden from us in the busy days, but now asking that we explore it and discover its resources, for it is a place where great energy has accumulated and waits to be tapped. When we are quiet, alone by day or unsleeping by night, a voice comes, inviting still deeper quietness – "Be still," it says, "and know that I am God." Keeping our stillness, the infinite I AM speaks again. "I am the living bread." "Take, eat." "I am the water of life." Drink and the living water will well up in you so that you can give it to the thirsty children. "I am the light of the world." Light your candle from the great flame of God's love, attend to its burning in your life, and the little ones will bring their candles for you to light them from your flame. "I am the good shepherd", but you and I will also receive the shepherd's crook and be able to lead and to rescue. The way, the truth, the life?

> Without the way there is no going
> Without the truth there is no knowing
> Without the life there is no living

Through this listening in silence, we find the practice of meditation. It costs nothing, only be still and aware of the great I AM. Keep aware of the breathing, the in and out of the breath. Be still and know. All life, remember, is taking, and holding, and giving again, so as you eat the living bread, drink the water of life, and find the way, you will be able to give to the hungry, the thirsty, the lost, and God will acknowledge your giving, so that the gate of death will open into His eternal Kingdom.

Some of us, working with our dreams, are also finding the way. An infinity of resource waits to be accepted, spiritual energy beyond our conceiving. "Only be strong and work for I am with you, saith the Lord of Hosts."

These days of unemployment, when so many almost hourly are losing their jobs and finding themselves out of work, should rally us to consider whether the words wake and work are almost synonymous. In the Scriptures, both Old and New Testament writers lay great stress on work as a creative function. God the Creator is at work in the universe and in our lives. Keeping the Jerusalem Bible translation in mind, we read, "God co-operates," "We are God's work of art," "We are God's garden." Jesus, speaking as Logos, says, "The father worketh and I work," and it is not difficult to find many behests to wake out of sleep. Can we hear the call to the sleepyheads who want, and think they need, 'a little-more slumber and a little more sleep'.

A first reaction to losing one's job, finding oneself unemployed, may well be, 'I shall be able to sleep, no alarm clock now', but shortly that becomes boring and a call to work greatly welcomed.

A job is defined in Chambers Dictionary as "an undertaking with a view to profit". The Oxford Etymological reference is to a cartload, and this gives rise to the question, positive or negative – a cartload of grain at harvest time, or a cartload of dirt? (Have you been in Canada on Garbage Sunday, when the winter's rubbish is deposited outside the house to be collected by the stout, able-bodied road-men with their enormous carts, clearing out the accumulation of stuff that has become useless, no longer needed. I wonder if these men are singing "The winter has passed and the spring come again.")

The Oxford book suggests a link between work and ergon and energy – that concept which we find mysterious, undefined, and yet limitless in what it accomplishes. The job has been lost. We have been thankful to sleep in the mornings, but now it is high time to awaken and ask ourselves what work is awaiting us, what opportunity is beckoning. 'Can I reorganise my days and my life, and do what I have always wanted to do?' 'I have always wanted to paint, to be an artist.' 'I have always wanted to make music.' 'Small children have always interested me.' 'I seem to have a longing to get to know old people.' 'Blind people stir my sympathy. I have often thought they might be glad if someone would read to them' 'There is an invalid woman living in my street. Do you think she would let me do her shopping?' 'When, I wonder, can I make a start?' The answer is NOW and the location, the place, is HERE. Take advantage of even the meanest opportunity, and other doors will open. Full employment awaits you when you are willing.

We repeat, the good life consists in taking, holding and giving again. Your energy has its source in THAT more than yourself and is waiting to be used. Hold it, and watch for the smallest opportunity, then let it work and you will find life joyful again, as it was when as a child you knew what you wanted.

We cannot over-estimate the necessity of 'plugging in', of being in contact with the Infinite Source, of keeping this alive, welling up in our spirits. It is imperative that there should be outlets for this life force within us, an awareness of the deprivation of others, so that our energy is directed towards the world's hunger and need.

(*c. 1980*)

All we have willed, or hoped or dreamed of good shall exist;
Not its semblance, but itself; no beauty, nor good, nor power
Whose voice has gone forth, but each survive for the melodist
When eternity affirms the conception of an hour.
The high that proved too high, the heroic for earth too hard,
The passion that left the ground to lose itself in the sky,
Are music sent up to God by the lover and the bard;
Enough that he heard it once: we shall hear it by-and-by.

From: "Abt Vogler" – *Robert Browning*

# The Elderly

When men and women come into their fortieth years, the fifth decade of their lives, they are likely to find their younger friends look on them as elderly. I well remember, when I was about forty years old, a lass in her twenties referring to "old people like you and your husband". It must have been soon afterwards that I found a 'Thought for the Day' on a tear-off calendar, an anonymous offering: "Men should know they are growing old not by the frailty of the body, but by the strength and creativity of the spirit."

Since then, many years have passed, and a wise friend, whom I have never met in the flesh, writes to urge me to value the tenth decade of my life. He affirms that most who have lived their lives well, by which he means those who have lived in loving relationship with their fellows, have great opportunity in quite unconscious ways to bring blessing into the community in which they live, and indeed to a wider circle.

When testing children to measure their innate intelligence, their chronological age is noted: how many years does their life span? Then the mental age is assessed: what have they been able to learn in the time given? A third measurement might well be that of emotional age. Even people with grey hair may have halted far back in infancy or childhood in their capacity to feel. This is a serious loss, since the early emotions of childhood are immature, raw and primitive. The repression is severe when the child is discouraged or disapproved should he exhibit his feelings, whether angry or loving, or if, alert in his curiosity, he is told that he 'asks too many questions,' or when, itching to feel shapes and textures, he is met with 'Don't touch!' Water play and mud pies keep a child happily for hours, but is he allowed to get wet and dirty?

When the instinctual needs are not understood by parents and their surrogates, but disapproved and disallowed, we get the repression which, if severe, makes for dull, disinterested children, who become the despair of their teachers as the years pass by with their opportunities for growth and learning missed. We owe a great debt to Maria Montessori who, with her insistence on the need to provide material and opportunity early in life, opened up new paths in education and the development of skills. It is obviously important to look for the secret of maintaining the energy which will keep us from ageing. It may not be one secret but several, and in the pages that follow we will be casting some light on them.

Let us think of ourselves as four-square. In dreams, we frequently dream of space so framed: the market square, the college quad, the swimming pool. In psychology, we are taught wisely by Jung to relate this to the four functions which, if integrated into our personality, make us whole people. Two of these functions, intuition and sensation, belong to all living creatures. Intuition is an awareness, knowing without the intervention of thought. Sensation is contact with the environment through the body: touching, hearing, seeing, smelling, tasting.

As life has developed and evolved, the contact between parent and offspring has led to the development of the feeling function. At first it is the awakening of tenderness. A bird gathers her chicks under her wings and attacks the intruder who would interfere with her brood. Reptiles and fish also lay eggs, but with them there is no development of tenderness since they keep no contact with their young. Love is dependent on this contact at the beginning of life. So vulnerable and probably so fear-ridden is the emergent creature that the parents must shelter and protect it, and defend it against the onslaught of enemies. Mammals and marsupials show the same feelings which, in human beings, we recognize as love and hate.

The fourth function, that of thought, is apparently peculiar to mankind: only man thinks. The human forebrain with its capacity to reason, to choose, to make decisions, has developed through thousands of years and replaces in function the olfactory lobes of the four-footed mammals. They kept their noses close to the ground and were guided by the sense of smell, of which only relatively weak traces survive in present-day man. Man's ability to think and reason has led to a vast accumulation of knowledge, a great world of science has been built up, and it has led to every kind of human activity involving tools and instruments, from Adam's spade to the Palomar Observatory and the nuclear bomb. But all this can easily be at the expense of the earlier, more primitive functions of life, bringing a crippling loss in the personality of the individual. It is the cultivation of our *four* sidedness which enables us to grow into maturity of spirit, and to make light of the inevitable decrease in bodily strength which old age brings.

In order to grow old wisely, cheerfully and without regrets, I suggest that we do not allow ourselves to give up the use and the enjoyment of our four-sidedness. Intuition is likely to persist longer than reason, as it is deeply rooted in life. Under the name of 'hunch' it is common to all and we should not lightly discard it, but rather trust our hunches and at times, even give them precedence over rational knowledge. In old age, with failing memory and diminished sight and hearing, we can keep to this inner wisdom of the psyche, sharing it as we do with children and primitive peoples.

Sensation, too, may be cultivated even with failing eyesight or hearing. The hand with its sensitive fingers need never lose the pleasure of contact with things rough or smooth. A firm, hard grasp makes for safety, and we can express much love and tenderness by touch and gesture. Is it only our imagination that makes us find the scent of roses and honeysuckle and ever-increasing joy?

And what of the heart function, our ability to feel? It is sad that modern, civilized life-patterns have tended in this twentieth century to lead us to deny the value of feeling, placing greater emphasis on the need to think. Feeling is repressed as unacceptable when children are told to keep a stiff upper lip. Boys in particular are discouraged from weeping and if they happen to do so are labelled soft or girlish. Professional women, too, are warned against letting their feelings get the upper hand. Young nurses in our hospitals are, all too often, told that there is no time to waste in giving sympathy to their patients. I clearly remember a dream that came to me when I was beginning to understand this conflict between the heart and the intellect. In my dream I was on board a great liner on its way from Bombay to London, passing through the Straits of Messina. We had crossed the depths of the Indian Ocean and the Red Sea. We had found the Suez Canal adequate to take the great ship, and had come across the deep Mediterranean in safety. Now we were approaching Marseilles, where I would disembark, soon to find myself in London again, committed to professional duties. As I watched from the prow, I was horrified to see the shallowness of the water. Since, in the dream, water is a symbol for feeling, I took the dream as a powerful warning not to sacrifice feeling and become immersed only in thinking, learning and professional work. It had a great influence on my life, because I was just beginning the experience and practice of psychoanalysis, and needed to remember that in straitened circumstances we must depend on feeling rather than thought. I like to remember the dream as positive. The captain on the bridge saw me through.

We are left with the fourth function: what of thought? It was the last to be developed in the course of evolution, and is vulnerable for that reason. A blow on the head, a glass too much alcohol, and we are incapable of thought. Intense emotion is also liable to deprive us of our ability to think, as in states of panic, infatuation or great suffering.

Our interest in this paper is focussed on the ageing process, and the question of whether the psyche need deteriorate because the physique is weakening. We are keeping in mind the four-squaredness, and the need to maintain the use of all four functions throughout our lives. Let us consider how best we can maintain and possibly widen this, and in so doing enrich the quality of the closing years. Let me share with you what I have learned.

Undoubtedly we need to take account of our genetic inheritance as well as of our earthly nature, and realize that some of us are more gifted with one or other of these four capacities, intuition, sensation, feeling and thought, than with the others. This need neither be a reason for envy nor for despair: we can still determine to use and cultivate as much as possible in our personalities for as long as possible.

In order to develop intuition at any age in life, we should learn to become more aware and more trustful of our hunches. We might tell someone about it when they come true, or even keep a notebook to record them. If we trust our hunches, we shall un-doubtedly discover that they are trustworthy.

For the sensation function, the advice to anyone longing to maintain it might well be 'Keep your hand in', which would mean that no skill should be lost prematurely for lack of use. Cooking, gardening and knitting can be practised in old age, as well as pain-ting, music-making, sketching and other uses of the hand.

What about the heart, with its function of giving love and care? Quite deliberately and consciously we can decide to practise the 'law of love' which involves us in the giving and taking of relation-ships: through my own experience I can testify that to give love brings love. There are gestures and words that we can still use, and deeds that we can still do whatever our age, with which to foster the great rewards of friendship. We do not need to hold to the childish idea of 'best' or 'special' friends. An individual life broadens and flows when it is full of caring for others. We should know ourselves as conduits, through which psychic energy can flow from the Source out into the life of humanity. I have quoted before some beautiful words from the apocryphal book of Ecclesiasticus:

"I go to water my orchard, to irrigate my flowerbeds, and see!
– the conduit has become a river, and the river a sea."

How best can we maintain the most recent function, our thinking? We can endeavour to keep in contact with ideas through books and by talking to people, always being open and ready to consider ideas that are not immediately acceptable. Scientists who are concerned with the actual workings of the brain inform us of the inevitable loss of our grey cells with the passing of time. We are forced to admit that the process of *learning*, that is, the capacity for acquiring knowledge, slows down. To learn a poem by heart can be a simple task in schooldays, but increasingly difficult in old age, although by no means impossible. To overcome this difficulty, and to find oneself still able to acquire fresh passages of poetry and prose in memory brings great pleasure. To make a habit of doing this may well retard the process of memory-deterioration, which can seem so wounding to one's self-respect. The admission of the mature student to our universities, and the recent establishment of the Open University offer valuable opportunities for people no longer young. Good teachers encourage their pupils, and avoid subjecting them to discouragement. All wise parents know this. How can we get the encouragement we need in old age? Others may encourage us, and we must encourage ourselves. If we expect great things of ourselves and of others even in old age, we shall be rewarded. We can still endeavour to live by the essential formula: 'Take, hold and give again.'

In his teaching on auto-suggestion, Coué maintained that we should avoid the use of the negative, and always make positive statements instead. For instance, at bedtime, if we avoid the 'not' in 'I shall not wake up tired in the morning', and say instead 'I shall wake up as fresh as paint in the morning', then our minds are likely to heed and our bodies to respond. This is likely to be a significant factor as, by making a habit of this way of thinking and talking, we can establish an optimism which will affect not only ourselves, but also the others whom our lives touch. Whether or not we attain a happy old age must to a great extent depend on our ability to relate to our neighbours caringly and in a spirit of optmism, and to be content to live in the here and now without anticipating trouble ahead, but always with the assurance that ALL WILL BE WELL.

(1982)

# Creativity in Later Life

In our lives, the dependence of childhood gives way to the interdependence of adult life but in old age dependence again looms ahead, often causing great anxiety. Who is to care for us when we can no longer manage the once simple business of daily existence? We search, perhaps, for possibilities that reassure us. What about sons, daughters, grand-children or someone else still young and strong? It doesn't seem the right answer, since all too often a son or daughter tending their aged parent has slid into a backwater of life and lost the opportunity of creative living. However devoted the service, it still has its shadow of resentment, leading so frequently to a crippling of life when death of the one who has imprisioned them sets them free.

The problem is being faced and tackled on behalf of the aged by organisations offering sheltered housing in one form or another. The Welfare State, strained badly at its seams, is ultimately responsible – or so we hope. Independence has often to be struggled for in early days. Children, even as infants, show a tendency to take things out of their parents' hands, attempting tasks too difficult for them. The wise parent honours this desire and need to be of use, and as time passes gives more responsibility so that a strong independence is allowed to develop. 'No, no, let Daddy do it' – the impatience and superiority of Daddy are even more crushing than the words. Patience, let us remind ourselves, is listed as one of 'the fruits of the spirit', a quality that can develop in a parent who loves his child.

Sad to say, in some quarters independence in childhood is frowned upon. Adults are more skillful and the work seems better done. Independence too may lead the child into dangers – but so does dependence when the prop is removed. Independent children learn to think for themselves. They develop initiative, they learn how to help others.

Old age is a second childhood and again we see the struggle for independence, when too much care is lavished on the old man or woman, as the case may be. This anxiety to protect, to be helpful,

to lend an arm, can be tiresome and irritating when the person involved, in spite of chronological age, is still able to control life.
The helpfulness may well be motivated by unconscious desires,
unrecognised wishes. 'Anxiety covers the unexpressed wish' is
difficult to take to heart but let us own up that sometimes at least
'I wish you were dead' is replaced by 'Do allow me to care for you'.

The habit of independence will not arrive suddenly in old age.
Its roots may well be planted in the earliest days and grow with the
years into adulthood when 'I can do it', 'Yes, I can manage' are the
words of useful members of society blessed with a sense of equality, the sense that as human beings we are neither inferior nor
superior to others in skill or human functioning. An army cannot
march well if one soldier leans on another's shoulders; but wound-
ed men must own up to their disabilities and allow stretcher-
bearers to do the work for which they are in readiness.

Inferiority plunges us into a ditch out of which we may be
unable to climb. Superiority sets us on a pedestal off which it is
easy to fall. The equality of the highroad should be granted to old
people and we need not anticipate their days of helplessness.
Young children and old folk all need opportunities for usefulness.
They need to be encouraged, not pushed aside because of
slowness, valued for what they can teach. As well as the aged,
children have much wisdom when allowed freedom to listen to
their own instinctual 'I want' and not handed over to the demand
that they should just sit still and not be a nuisance. Their life will
blend with the other lives around them and bring blessing.

A friend of mine well on in her eighties insisted on living alone.
Her one daughter had married and lived abroad. Neighbours and
busybodies seemed anxious about her. What if . . .? and there were
many possibilities boding disaster. Providence was kind and she
died peacefully in her bed with no sign of struggle. What then is
Providence? I can only guess that the more we allow ourselves to
depend on it the more sure we become of its existence. Through
all the ages, and everywhere in the world, man has from the beginning postulated that there are 'gods'. In our day the certainty of
Life, the Spirit, not dependent on material things, discarding the
body when done with but surviving it, is acceptable in varied faiths
throughout the world. In their own way perhaps everyone,
everywhere, believes in Providence. A deep-seated instinct urges us
to appeal for help and succour when we come to the limits of our
ability.

The teaching of St. Paul, following on St. John's awareness of

'Logos' uniquely present in the man Jesus during his earthly ministry, has great psychological significance. Before his death, anticipating new life, resurrection and unity with the divine spirit in which there is no death, Jesus, now speaking as Logos, makes the promise to his disciples, and to us who follow, that he is eternally present in our lives.

Hippies talk of vibes, short for vibrations. In the academic environment we puzzle over a possible definition of energy. In religious and mystical circles the word spiritual leads us into the non-material world. 'In the Beginning God.' In the beginning energy? Teilhard de Chardin in his *Phenomenon of Man*, dealing with evolution, postulates 'sub-atomic dust' as the basis of the lithosphere, the world of rocks on which the world of life is built. Teilhard uses the symbolism of water to help us to understand the changes brought about by evolution. The atoms of hydrogen and oxygen combine to make a new element. As ice this is hard, solid, immobile. With warmth it melts and flows. The stream moves, no longer inert. When it comes in contact with heat its temperature rises and the water becomes steam, a great source of energy. So,we are taught this is happening in the world of nature. The 'sub-atomic dust' is energy – it takes on the shape and texture of material objects – earth, stones, crystals and then – a critical point – the non-living has changed and is alive. The great tree of life planted in the good earth branches and spreads. Vegetation develops and coincidentally, for they are interdependent, animal life. Wind and tide scatter the seed of plants but the animal race is mobile and travels far.

The ocean is the great mother of all living things but so slight is our capacity for seeing this, that we remain unaware, unconscious of its teeming diverse forms of life; conscious only of what is happening on its surface and on dry land. How limited, let us reflect, is that consciousness. The mobility of the animal hastens the development of skill, of knowledge, of relationship. An important discovery that four feet are not necessary for going places led to the liberation of the hand. Much followed, a forebrain developed, giving the creature a capacity for choice, decision making, the birth of thought. And so the race of man is established. Only man thinks. From then on the emergence of a new form of energy is liberated in the world. The power to create and the ability to destroy have taken on immense dimensions which with passing time increase and accelerate in their growth.

Today's question is 'Will spiritual energy with increasing power take hold of life as we know it?' The answer must be 'Yes, since the movement is there and the spirit beckons mankind ahead'. But we cannot guess or know whether great waves of destruction are imminent and what aeons may have to be travelled before the end, before the Alpha of the sub-atomic energy has been transmuted into the Omega of spiritual energy, omnipotent and everlasting.

Insistently the question forces itself upon us, 'What can I do? Can I conceivably have even one thread in my hand, one pebble, small, almost invisible?' Yet there is interweaving and many pebbles on every beach. Individual service, individual effort, is puny but each individual carries responsibility for the here and now of his life. The infinitely small virus can destroy a strong man's life but how little do we know and recognise the factors creating the awaited crisis when the material will give place to the spiritual, when water flows as ice melts – when the energy of steam takes over from the frozen Arctic ice. We have to be content to not-know when, but each individual laying hold on life hastens that day.

"Glory be to Him whose power working in us does infinitely more than we can ask or imagine.' Thank you, St. Paul, for your vision and faith. You have told us that we are only earthenware jars to hold the treasure. The treasure is that Spirit, other than our mortal own, to whose power we can set no limit.

(*1982*)

Put love in and you will draw love out"

*St. John of the Cross*

# The Unexpected and the Unconscious

I had been asked to speak to a group of students and given as the title of my talk "The Unexpected" – I added "and the Unconscious", since my work as an analyst lies in this field. Unconscious means *not knowing*. We do not know what is going to happen from one moment to the next. *To expect* – its Latin root is *spectare* to look and we use the same root in spectacle, spectacular, respect, conspectus. So to expect is to look out for, almost to obtain by this activity. The Bible is full of this word, particularly the Old Testament. The Jews *expected* a Messiah, they waited *expectantly* for a new age, the age of salvation. *Unexpected* things happen to us all in the course of life, and we are constantly confronted with events which may be better or worse than anything we ever expected.

I wish to relate this to the matter of the KOAN – which is a problem that seems insoluble, a question for which there seems no answer. When a Buddhist teacher accepts a disciple, a learner of his wisdom, he gives him a Koan with the instruction that he meditate upon it continually, disregarding the apparent impossibility of finding the answer. One such Koan is "This is the sound of two hands clapping. What is the sound of one hand clapping?". There are many Koans, and a too clever American is said to have published a book with all the answers. The answer, however, is individual. It must emerge from the deep unconscious of the disciple's mind. He must hope and *expect* to find it through meditation. Not expecting the answer he still expects *something to happen* – light breaks in from the unconscious. Three examples of this came to mind as I planned how best I could give a message to these students (who incidentally, I hope *expected* that I would open their minds to some fresh aspect of the truth!).

KOAN 1 Here is the setting of the first Koan – Earthquake in Turkey at the beginning of winter. Tragic stories were coming to us over the radio – snow on the mountains. . . . leaving their old houses....old people and children were exposed to the wintry cold. What could I do? Money – blankets – food – too little – too late. I was a member of a meditation workshop in the Salisbury Centre that day – the instructions were only be quiet, watch your breathing. A blizzard outside – snow – wind and darkness. Suddenly I thought of Max and Mitch – motor cyclist and pillion passenger. How were they to get back to Fife in the darkness and storm? *Of course* – I could do something – I had no spare room, but a couch, and a mattress could be laid on the floor – blankets? Yes and a downie. Food – well yes it could be found – there is always something in the fridge. So I told them what I hoped they could do. Mitch said "Marvellous, Winifred that really is good" but Max said "Not at all, we'll both go home in the train". So they went, but my *caring thought* had been willing to upset my routine that night and take them in. Unexpected solution to my caring for the strangers in Turkey. Unexpected refusal, but I had been willing. Not the people on the Turkish mountains, but my neighbours – my willingness, my caring, was the answer.

KOAN 2 Jess is married to a sadist – a man to whom sex has no connotation of love, but only of inflicting suffering on the object of his relatedness. In the course of analysis we realised that she had never loved her husband – had married him to get a home of her own away from her unloving parents. Her relationship to her husband was insecure. He had extramarital affairs and was irresponsible towards her and her three young children. She became aware of the lack of love in herself, but also of other lacks – she had no aggression. This is – like sexual love – one instinctual element of psychic energy without which we become lethargic and uninteresting. Aggressive? Nasty aggressive creature? but the root of the word gives a clearer meaning *ad* = towards – *gressus* = a step.

So without aggression we do not step out towards the husband, the mate, the neighbour – Jess began to realize that in her married life she had become a doormat – inert – an object for her husband's compulsive sexual activity which was completely devoid of love and elicited no love in her. She had originally come for help in the situation not for herself or for her husband but because Jack, her eight year old son was stammering badly and all three children were friendless and doing badly at school. She saw the *boy's stammer* as an insoluble problem. Two different child guidance clinics had been consulted but the necessary help was unavailable. Jess kept her attention fixed on Jack – his stammer. No help – no betterment – no way out. Months and years passed with apparent deterioration. The husband's cruelty was hard to bear, and as the children got older they copied their father in rejecting and humiliating her.

Something *unexpected* happened. The husband had been more than ever unkind, taunting her with some undeserved fault – doormat indeed? She lifted a plate of hot yellow curry which she had put at his place on the table and threw it in his face. The amazing result was that *he* apologised for what he had said and did not apparently resent her action. It was a turning point in their relationship. Slowly but surely it improved, they began to know what life can mean – when lived with understanding and love. For years divorce had seemed to be the only alternative to the doormat marriage, but it too seemed impossible. The husband would not consent to her leaving him nor to giving her custody of the children. As their mother she could not contemplate leaving them to a father who was undependable and often cruel in his attitude to them – often *insoluble* seemed the word written over her marriage situation. *Unexpected*? Who could have thought it would be solved by her aggressive act and that plate of hot curry?

KOAN 3 When I began my work as an analyst I thought of analysis as a pretty certain cure of neurotic illness. The neurotic symptoms *are* the seven deadly sins:

Pride: over compensation for inferiority
Sloth: no energy, the libido is blocked
Envy: in relationship to parents and older siblings
Anger: frustration
Jealousy: lack of self-esteem
Greed: over-compensation for lack of love
Lechery: over-emphasis of the physical from lack of love

I see them all now as the outcome of deep-seated anxiety, the spirit of fear engendered in the insecurity of early childhood – perhaps even before birth, but I believed that if we worked hard enough on analysis the patient would recover.

Many did, and, moreover, astonished me by developing creativity which brought with it happiness, joy, light-heartedness which gladdened the heart. My patients who had never owned a paint box became artists – one exhibited in a picture show in less than a year – another won a prize in a poster exhibition. A third bought a piano for £5 and found she could begin again at thirty where she left off at twelve years old. A man developed a pretty wit when he got rid of his inhibitions. They had been imposed by an older brother who said "You think you are funny do you?". Another wrote poetry and yet another found the gift of public speaking. So it went on – *but* every now and again the Koan, the insoluble problem strayed into my consulting room and lay down on the analytic couch. Sometimes the patient was the victim of obsessively compulsive behaviour – deep-rooted – apparently inaccessible. At other times I met the deeply depressed person rejected even in his mother's pregnancy: 'I never wanted that child!' Occasionally I could not but wonder if the terrible depression and self-loathing were not a manifestation of karma, that is of dark happenings carried over from previous lives. In the belief in reincarnation we are forced to accept the hypothesis "As a man sows so shall he reap". These Koan patients however have their own virtue and their own value to the analyst:

1. Firstly, they puncture his hubris, his omnipotence, which is so serious a fault in his profession, and send him back to find his own centre of energy and ability, in the certainty that he must work with the co-operation of the unconscious life-forces. Put in religious terms he must be certain of the "Not I, but Christ". Faced with the so-called 'hopeless case' he must realise over and over again that hope is an anchor of the soul and keeps us in touch with the Source of all healing. Psychologically it keeps us doggedly in touch with the patient's needs.

2. Secondly the patient may hold on like grim death to his/her symptom, inducing despair in the unbelieving analyst. In the depth, however, something is happening. The wound is healing from the depth – as all good surgeons expect. Meantime the symptom maintains its function and brings the patient to the physician and when they part the symptoms too disappear – unexpected!!

3. These Koan patients undoubtedly not only make great demands upon the analyst, but as a reward they elicit in him fresh gifts of intuitive wisdom. They constantly refer him back to the resource of his own unconscious, so that it is not the easy straightforward case that teaches him his trade but the perverse

difficult negative patient with whom he has to grapple and from whom he learns most – learns to be patient, to be faithful, to control his anger when he is abused and to keep a certainty that God not the Devil is in charge. *Amor vincit Omnia.* "God is there" – Jung in his old age carved on his door post – "Whether we call him or not".

I am grateful to have been given the title for this talk – *The Unexpected – The Unconscious.* The unconscious has infinite dimensions and we impoverished mortals live apparently only in four: three of space and one of time. Let us keep aware, groping in the darkness for the light, retrieving from the unconscious the creative gifts that are our birthright – so that we too fulfil the purpose underlying all evolution, more consciousness, more creativity – we co-operate with the eternal Purpose. How strange that St Paul wrote to the Roman Christians nearly 2000 years ago that "God co-operates with those who are called according to His Purpose".

(*c. 1973*)

Say not the struggle naught availeth
The labour and the wound in vain
The enemy fainteth not nor faileth
And as things have been they remain

If hopes were dupes, fears may be liars
It may lie in you smoke concealed
Your comrades chase e'en now the fliers
And but for you, possess the field

For while the tired waves vainly breaking
See here no nich to gain
For back through creeks and inlets breaking
Comes silent, flooding in, the main

And not by eastern windows only
When daylight comes, comes in the light
In front the sun climbs slow, how slowly
But westward look the land is bright.

*E. A. Clough*

# Art and the Unconscious

Pictures and images are all-important in our dreams, sometimes, it is true, we hear words, something is said, even at times a bell rings to waken us, to alert us perhaps to another level of dreaming or to awaken us to consciousness. The image, however, is the staple content – landscapes, vehicles, all manner of things and people. The dream produces scenes which surprise us by their unexpected strangeness and their vivid presentation, and their relevance is disturbing when we are able to connect them not only to childhood perhaps, but also to the present moment.

Scientists, denying what cannot be 'taped', recorded, and reproduced, have been inclined to doubt the work of the early analysts, pioneers in the study of unconscious processes affecting our lives. Freud's early discoveries came from studying cases of hysteria with conversion symptoms; Jung's patients with schizophrenia, and Groddeck's with 'incurable' illness. Each of these teaches us to be aware of factors, causative, although not easily recognised, of strange symptoms, aberrant processes of thought and behaviour, and gross physical illness. Freud and Jung, and their schools have given great importance to dreams as carriers of information from this unknown area of man's being, centered in sleep.

As recently as the early 1940s the electricial energy of the brain's activity was 'taped' and the differing waves recorded during the periods of waking, sleeping and dream-sleep. More recent research has shed light on the alternating modes of psychic activity according to the functioning of right and left hemispheres of the brain. It must remain a strange anomaly that mankind have used their energy, time and money to explore the moon and outer space before they had accurate knowledge of what has happening within the living brain – so important a part of their own physical being.

By using observation and the recording of electro-magnetic activity we now know that babies dream, long continuous dreams. The textbooks state that old people's dreams are scanty, but from my own observations and experience I can deny the reliability of this statement, and assert that, in my nineties I am still dreaming vividly. So far as I know we have not yet a method of discovering whether the unborn infant dreams, and if so, whether he dreams about movement, contact and sound – all part of pre-natal experience. It seems unlikely that he dreams in images. I am told that people blind from birth have no pictures in their dreaming.

Picture making, we can guess, is a function of interplay between the conscious and unconscious aspects of the psyche and that without physical vision there are no dream images. Lacking dream images is it possible that our capacity to project the image and create art forms would be inhibited? Have you ever been startled on waking by a beautiful object in a dream and the realisation that *you* must have created it? It is not unusual for dreamers to report such a situation, involving them in a wonder at their artistic creativity. We have to ask is it there all the time in the unconscious, this wonderful ability to depict form and colour and to create beauty? I have been told by instructors in art that the apparently fotuitous gift for art, genetic, inherited it may be, seems to be of less importance than a determination to find the way of expression. We are reminded that genius has been described as 'an infinite capacity for taking pains'. But is this determination to get it right truly art? Is this not a focussing on the external that we see with the outer eye?

May I take you now, not into a school, but into a studio into which people venture as if by chance. Paper or some other surface is provided, paints and pigments of many sorts, brushes; you may bring the pigment to the paper in any way you choose – 'let the brush do it all', without the *determination to get it right*. Later perhaps a rag, sponge, or the fingers bring the surface closer to the painter. *Something is happening* – bringing relaxation and pleasure as we paint, and gradually colours and shapes, maybe textures, emerge to create something that satisfies.

The spontaneous work of young children has been adequately studied and its developement noted. The words so insistently used in early childhood 'I want', denoting the activity of the libido includes the wish to be an agent of image-projection. How precarious the fate of the early 'want', 'need','desire' may be, can be understood when you visualize and understand the experience of a three year old child who came as a patient in her thirties suffering from depression and threatening signs that the dreaded split in personality was a possibility. Debby at the age of three had a baby brother. She told me with great excitment at the recollection, how her mother one day went out shopping, leaving her with baby boy in his pram out in the garden. She became aware that something was happening under the coverings and put her hand in to investigate. She withdrew it (I use her own words) "covered with lovely yellow stuff". The outside polished surface of the pram plainly offered itself for decoration. There was plenty of 'stuff' and plenty of time to do a really splendid painting. *But* Mother, on her return from the shops, took a very poor view of her daughter's artistic creation. She was smacked, scolded and warned *never to do such a thing again*. When Debby came to see me this prohibition was still operating – she told me she had *never wanted to paint*. When the impulse was released, the painting began and really beautiful pictures were created. In the first watercolour landscape the smearing impulse was evident as the clouds were depicted as if impressed by a continous wavy movement. Within a short time Debby's pictures were accepted for exhibition in an art gallery and her creativity took many fresh directions.

I am no authority on art or surrealism, but I would suggest that Debby's use of this primitive pigment, the first colourful thing man creates, and the direct contact of *hand* with the outside surface of things, was at the time powerfully exciting. Mother had gone away, so that she was free for the time being from the prohibiting 'ought not' of the super-ego. 'Plenty of it', of time as well as material, liberated the urge to paint. The violence of the maternal prohibition acted as a deterrent to the impulse for thirty years. How clearly this story illustrates the return of repressed material, unaffected by the experience of intervening years. In Debby's case deep-freezing provides a wonderful modern symbolism; the talent emerges unaffected by time. Other deterrents may well spring to your mind, perhaps from your own experience. One may be 'Hand me the brush and I'll show you' or just a giggling parent or sibling who makes fun of what you produced.

Music and other art forms present themselves precariously to begin with. A child who won't play the piano or cannot handle a stringed instrument may find himself creative with a reed or a pipe. I might again quote Alfred Adler "Parents must *always* encourage their children. Discouragement they will meet on every hand as they face the world. *Parents must never hesitate to encourage*".

The persistent image, preceding the word, demands of us that we use it as a means of communication. There is a great loss to ourselves, perhaps even to mankind, if we do not use it as a means of contact with others. *Look* – be aware, conscious, mindful of what you see – far more than you ever thought was there – movement, shape, colour all speak to us of what is happening. Wind moving the branches tell us of its spirit. Shape, form, structure speak of the stability, but also of the inherent instability of created things – and colour, not only apparent in the outer world, is there, too, in our dreams, intensifying our feeling and lifting our hearts.

Some of us have lost or have not developed the gift of picture making that is tangible, but we may still have intense inner vision which we can use as we talk to others of the mysteries. Some of us, visualizing the dreams of those who tell us what they have seen in their sleep, are given the insight to put their visions into words so that, both seeing and hearing, differing aspects of truth become obvious. Let us claim the birthright of the dreaming faculty – not losing the child's gift, but sharing the visions of the young and attending with thankfulness to the dreams of our old age.

Dreams demand attention and we by-pass them at our great loss. Those of us who are engaged in group dream work whether in this country, in the USA or elsewhere are very deeply convinced that more people should avail themselves of this opportunity of enlarging their experience and moving their horizons further afield. To share in the visualization of the dream-picture and develop insight into the language of the dream-image bring an increase of our own self-knowledge and a new and very precious way of relating to our neighbours.

(*1972*)

# Forgiveness & Healing

The causes of illness seem to be obvious – maybe some infection or poison in the food, some exposure to extremes of heat and cold; those certainly are factors of causation, but why we must ask are some of us so liable to illness and accident? I have even heard people boast that there is scarcely a bone in their body that has not at some time or other been broken in the course of their lives. We also hear people averring that they never escape influenza or other illnesses during epidemics. The words 'accident prone' have become commonplace. Some of our friends are always in trouble from some form of disability, apparently imposed from without. It is necessary, however, to ask ourselves whether there are internal, unconscious reasons why we fall ill.

Are we punishing ourselves, I wonder, unconsciously, and if so, why? In the Gospels, we learn of an invalid being brought to our Lord on a stretcher carried by four of his friends. He receives healing through Christ's assurance that his sins are forgiven him, and is immediately able to set his friends free from their burden, and to walk away healed, carrying his own stretcher.

Is it then our guilt, our fear of having done wrong, or sinning, for which the illness is punishing us? The patient indignantly may tell us, "I don't want to bring this illness upon myself. Do you think I would willingly give up pleasures to find myself sick in bed?" Or, "why is it that so often I get into trouble just at the time that I so want to enjoy life?"

The answer, of course, is not obvious, and does not lie in conscious awareness but is only to be understood when the deeper unconscious motivations of our conduct become plain. When Christ said, "Son, Thy sins are forgiven thee," it became explicit that his patient was suffering from unforgiven sin, in other words, that he was a guilty man. Do we not all bear this burden from early life onward? Human beings are subjected to disapproval of their conduct, are blamed for unapproved behaviour and made to feel guilty from early days.

It seems as if we try to make our children 'good' by showing them how wrong their behaviour is in our eyes. In modern psychology we try to convince parents that their task is not so much in demanding goodness, but rather in promoting the well-being and happiness of their children. Punishment and parental disfavour cannot but stir up resentment in a child's heart. This resentment must be understood as repressed hostility toward the parent, teacher or other authority figure. Are they indeed always in the right, and the child always in the wrong?

And so we find that from very early days we may be the unhappy victims of guilty feelings from which it seems impossible to rid ourselves. It is unlikely that we have any clue to their cause and origin, since as I have said they are repressed, and lie deep in the unconscious. Nowadays let us be thankful that understanding is growing, and moreover, that there is a possiblity of treatment through understanding and the discovery through analysis of how it all began.

Going back to the Old Testament, in Psalm 103 we have foretaste of Christ's teaching in "He pardoneth Thine iniquities, He healeth all our diseases". Let us accept the two statements as cause and effect, that forgiveness brings healing in its wake. What follows in the Psalm is reassuring, "He redeemeth Thy soul from destruction". How best can we understand the meaning of redemption? Let us envisage a household vessel that has been broken. What is to be done about it? Should we let it go, throw it into the ash-heap, or can it be mended and redeemed, that is, brought back into daily use?

How beautiful and reassuring are the words of the Psalm, "forgiveness brings healing", and when we are healed, we are again brought into full usefulness in God's service.

*(1983)*

"Atonement" – at onement.

# Spiritual Issues

## Diaspora

*"Slowly, but I believe inevitably, the integrating forces of the unconscious are at work quite beyond what we think or imagine."*

A word at times reverberates in the mind. "Can't get that word out of my head," we mutter. So it has happened to me with this Greek word which, in modern speech, has become 'dispersal'. Throw a stone into a pool and you don't know where the ripples end. Take 'flu or some other infection, sneeze hard, and you cannot guess at what distance the victims of your involuntary action may be. Whisper a word into your neighbour's ear. Taking hold of the idea, he may be teaching, preaching or writing about it with no memory of how it first entered his mind as important.

To look at our word with interest, Dia – through, spora – the scattering. Spores are germs that have gone into hiding. They take no account of time and it is difficult to guess what stimulus arouses them to new activity.

Do you, I wonder, sometimes speculate about the pre-historic civilization of Atlantis? Prehistory or myth – who can tell? The story goes that they developed scientific knowledge far in advance of ours today. They had discovered a way of releasing atomic energy, but had not learned to control it. When the great explosion occured Atlantis was destroyed, but a dispersal took place and fragments of Atlantean wisdom have possibly settled in Egypt, Babylon, Persia, China, India, Tibet, Mexico – who knows where the spores found an environment with the opportunity for growth. Lying dormant through the centuries, or even millennia, they await the stimulus through which life will germinate and something more will grow and become fruitful.

In Biblical times, we have the history of the Jewish dispersal to

Babylon. Did Monotheism, the knowledge of the one God, strike roots with lasting effects? In South India, a community of 'Thomas Christians' still persists. It is not clear whether the persecution of the early Church sent seeds scattering as far as that country or whether, as legend has it, St. Thomas himself founded the Church in that land.

In more recent times, Hitler was the agent of a great dispersal of psycho-analytic knowledge with the disruption of the Jewish communities in Vienna and Berlin. In Vienna in the nineteen-thirties, before Hitler came to power, clouds were gathering around the Jewish people. An ugly word, *unerwünscht*, unwelcome, greeted them on café doors. While Freud was carefully investigating his cases with their dreams, which resulted in the grasp we have today of unconscious processes, another physician, Alfred Adler, was urging those who would listen to him to consider what the true goal of life could be. His personal problem, being a small, undersized man and a Jew, made him aware of inferiority – that which makes us different from our fellows, constantly striving for equality or, disastrously, for superiority. With his family he fled before the approaching Hitler storm and found himself in New York where he attracted large audiences. Here again is *diaspora*. Freud and Jung visited the USA in the days of their friendship before the first World War. They must have sown the seeds or implanted the spores which developed in Adler's extraverted wisdom now affecting many in that country – the New World, who were ready to accept and disseminate what was still a new way of understanding the nature of human life. In this preparation of the ground, credit should also be given to the Scotsman, William MacDougall who, as professor at Duke University in North Carolina, had given a fundamental teaching about man's instinctual life.

In the life-time of many who read this, it is as if a great flood of wisdom from the deep unconscious has swept through the USA – beginning by infection – a sneeze from Vienna finding a favourable environment, a nidus, in New York, in Chicago and the Middle West, and then deploying itself along the whole Californian coast – gaining vigour as it spread.

We, in Britain, took very little notice of how valuable it would have been for us to retain more of these analysts. Were we, perhaps, afraid of the fact that it was, on the whole, the Jews who were responsible for the spread of this work? Nowadays we are,

I hope, envious of what is happening out West, and avail ourselves of the teaching as it becomes possible. What about Tibet and the dispersal of the monks with their awareness of the ancient truths? Scotland was fortunate in being able to welcome them and allow them to establish a monastery near Dumfries where the practice of meditation took root and has grown, almost unobserved, into a great tree. From Thailand, also, a great dispersal has taken place. Dhiravamsa and Tew Bunnag have given us so much. Chapter House, their centre, has its opportunities for learning continuously through the years with the wonderful book on non-attachment. The Bahai faith, Sufi teaching, deep wisdom from distant lands are available for our needs today. We are thankful, too, and sincerely acknowledge the truths that are coming to us from the depth psychology of the present day. Not only are we, as individuals, taking advantage of opportunities for psychoanalysis, but the Dream Analytic Movement is active with great possibility for expansion.

Whether we explore and reach the depths through meditation or through analytic methods, let us hope that the results are the same – liberation of our creative potential, freedom from anxiety, and involvement in the great movement in which something is always happening as the spirit takes over from the body. Of that Kingdom there shall be no end.

A friend came to visit me just as I had, so I thought, finished writing about Diaspora. I told her something of what I had been writing and she asked, "How does that fit into your book, *Ten Decades*? I thought it was autobiographical." I had been scribbling more or less compulsively during the days – not knowing until I started what I wanted to write – only in some way possessed by the word and its meaning. Now I see that it has to do with my tenth decade – a time of loss. Faced with the interpretation of a difficult dream, I reassure the dreamer that we must realise always that the dream is positive. Dreams of death? The unconscious is aware of life after life.We die that we may live and, without resurrection, death and life make no sense. I am writing on 31st December, 1981. The year is dying. Let it die. Tomorrow's New Year is bringing hope.

Has the year, 1981, been a year of Diaspora in my personal life? I have made many new friends. I think of three contacts with Japan, many in the USA. In Canada, loving links are still being forged with my grandchildren and their parents, and a new great-grandson is growing up in the Canadian far west. Wherever I look, friends come to greet me. Several interviews on the Radio have brought response – not only BBC, but Radio Forth and Radio Clyde have elicited new contacts. My daughter, Diana Bates, and I on Television as "friends" were warmly received, and why did one viewer reiterate that across the screen the word TRUTH was inscribed? My book *Something is Happening*, was published and its value has been acclaimed by old friends and new. "Glory be," I say, "to Him Whose Power working in us does infinitely more than we can ask or imagine." Has He made me a live wire to carry His Message, His Good News, out into a world beyond my ken? A bit of wire that has not been discarded but used – plugged into the Source; one of the many, innumerable ways in which the Living Word is transmitted. About fifty people each week attend Dream Analytic Groups at which I am present – one each day of the week except Sunday. Scarcity of available analysts brought these groups into being, and at first we thought of them as second best to one-to-one analysis. The reverse is proving to be the case, and there is real joy in the gatherings as we see so much happening. Members who have come sad and depressed, return one day with shining faces, reporting that something wonderful is happening in their lives. There is a great spirit of caring, of holding those in distress as we gather, and the energy of each increases and is multiplied in the healing process.

We set out with humility to investigate our dreams, but how much more happens! Healing and renewal of strength in the individual, better relationships in the family, an acceptance of the job provided in business. We see such changes taking place and our hearts are warmed when members contribute by their words, "Before I came to this group . . .; since I came to the group . . . ."

Slowly, but I believe inevitably, the integrating forces of the unconscious are at work quite beyond what we think or imagine. Diaspora? Am I, an old woman nearing the hundred years, breaking up? I am blind, barely seeing enough to write and unable at present to read. I am deaf, but hear enough to gather what the dreamers are communicating. However, this fragmentation must be accounted positive. Seeds are germinating, valuable spores are lying dormant, integral to dispersal, to the breaking up and scattering; to the words "Fear not. Lo! I am with you always, even to the end", and the reassurance, "In our end is our beginning."

(Appeared in *New Humanity* 1982)

# The Well

What do we find at the bottom of the well? A spring of water – *Ursprung-Quelle* – bubbling up from a deeper source. *Urgrund*, the ground of our being. The well is deep, but the reward is marvellous. Dig deep, dig with hope, dig with faith.

The well in Samaria where Jesus gave the supreme teaching of the nature of God, was dug by Jacob in an earlier time. He was Israel, aware of the presence of God at Bethel, but also the shepherd who dug wells, penetrating Mother Earth to her depths to obtain the flowing water which would 'slocken' (a Scots word meaning to relieve thirst) his thirsty sheep and irrigate the pastures to give them nourishment.

What lies at the bottom of the well? Truth. We dig deep to find it, exploring the Unconscious through the dream and meditation. It flows – Jung calls it *libido* – symbolised by the river. Vipassana Buddhists call it *intuitive wisdom*. Nietzsche's word was *life force*. Freud learnt from Groddeck to call it the *id*, the instinctual energy. In his writing, "The Book of the It", Groddeck attributes to the id that energy *That* which in its destructive aspect causes disease and injury, but in the creative brings healing and new life. Groddeck is called the father of psycho-somatic medicine, since he saw so clearly the link between physical illness and psychological misapprehension.

In the Old Testament, the symbolic flowing of water is used extensively, for example in Ezekiel, chapter 47, where we are told that the spring is at the east door of the Jerusalem temple, and the river flows irrigating the desert and bringing life to the Dead Sea. In the apocryphal Book of Ecclesiasticus, chapter 25, verses 42 and 43, "I am going to water my orchard. . . .to irrigate my flower beds. And see, my conduit has grown into a river, and my river has grown into a sea." Isaiah, chapter 58, verse 11, "You shall be like a watered garden, like a spring of water whose waters never run dry."

In the New Testament, Jesus the Christ as Logos identifies

himself with the flowing spring of water. John, chapter 7, verse 38, "If any man is thirsty, let him come to me. Let the man come and drink who believes in me. . . .From his breast shall flow fountains of living water." And at the well to the Samaritan woman, (John chapter 4, verse 14), "Anyone who drinks the water that I shall give will never be thirsty again; the water that I shall give will turn into a spring inside him, welling up to eternal life".

Returning to the well of Samaria and the woman, alien from the Jews, despised as promiscuous in her sex, and inferior because of her femininity, to her Jesus gave the supreme Logos teaching, (John, Chapter 4, verse 24), "God is spirit, and those who worship must worship in spirit and in truth."

In Laurens van der Post's early book, *Venture to the Interior*, he related the story of his mother's faith. After the death of her husband and the departure into the outer world of Laurens, one of her younger children, she decided to explore the possiblity of finding water on a property they owned on the edge of the Kalahari Desert. Taking with her a German governess, who had long been attached to the family, and an engineer, she set out into this area to discover whether water for irrigation was available. She had a complete belief that by digging she would come across the flow, but for long enough nothing happened. The engineer gave up hope of finding anything, and one day he decamped. However, this determined woman had the courage and the faith to find another engineer in a neighbouring town. No sooner was his digging begun than they were rewarded with a great upflow from the depths. The apparatus of pumps and pipes awaiting this discovery was ready to install, and soon the irrigation was established and the land became fruitful.

In my friendship with Sir Laurens, I became in some way identified with his mother and her certainty of resources in the depths. The process of psychoanalysis involves exploring the deep places of human personality. Analyst and analysand alike must have hope, trust and fidelity that leads to the result. With the analysis comes a release of energy, creative in its nature and surprising in its results: a very great reward to the faithful in this field.

In the Old Testament, there are many accounts of the digging of wells, and their function as a gathering place for the village people is often related. Ebenezer found a wife for Jacob among the maidens at the well. Jacob's well in Israel is still in existence, lying on the road between Haifa and Jerusalem. It is strangely unlike the well as our imagination would picture it, simply stone walls enclosing a structure. Nowadays, plastic is predominant in the bucket and the drinking vessel, but still the well is there, with water rising up as it has done through the centuries. In the depth of our being, the Unconscious, lies always that which is in touch with life's creativity; our ways of reaching it will change as ages pass, but our certainity of its existence must be allowed to dominate our lives.

A friend resident in Winchester tells me that in the crypt of that wonderful Cathedral lies a well which in times of flood may overflow, so that a river flows beneath the Cathedral. She relates that recently she joined a crowd of tourists, one of whom enquired of the Cathedral guide how frequently it was necessary to clean out the well. The answer was that the well is self-purifying and self-renewing with the constant flow from the clouds above to the depths and again rising to supply man's need. I am writing this at a time of industrial action, when the water supply of England and Wales is no longer to be taken for granted by the turning of a tap. Instead, members of many families are once again having to con-gregate at a central source to fill their buckets for the needs of the household. Can we guess that although this inflicts hardship, it may also be having positive value in bringing together people otherwise isolated? Also we may realise that when the taps are turned on again there will be a renewal of gratitude for something which for so long we have taken for granted. Once again the water will not need to be boiled to make it suitable for family use; it will come from the tap already purified to be used according to our need.

In the depths of the Unconscious lie the purifying forces which give us the security that comes from trusting life as God-given. He is faithful and supplies all our needs. We should have no doubt of *That* which flows into our lives, His will, the will of God, known to us as one with the love of God. Shall we use the petition "Give us this day our daily bread" with the meaning, give us contact to-day with the living bread, the bread of life. And so we hear the words "Take, eat" and you need never hunger.

(Appeared in *New Humanity*, 1983)

# Is a New Day Dawning

As I write this on January 10th, 1982, the daylight is almost imperceptibly, yet quite certainly, lengthening. The return from the darker days into Spring and Summer light has begun. My heart lights with thankfulness since not only in the outward happening does hopefulness stir, but the symbolism also revives the spirit. "Lighten our Darkness", we pray, and the answer comes, "Darkness is giving way to Light."

In my old age, approaching one hundred years, living alone in Edinburgh, I have a constant stream of visitors from different parts of the world and from different cultures. Easily, it seems, we slip away from 'chatter' into talking of deeper matters – the things of the spirit, the wisdom of the unconscious – this strange collective psyche which seems to be responsible for the many synchronicities we relate to each other. Many of my guests are psychic and talk to me of strange experiences. Others, like myself, are more earthly, but still we have our dreams, our expectations – energy, perhaps, with a longing to use it. Many of them tell me of an awareness that Edinburgh is a centre – probably one of many – where spiritual energy is gathering in preparation for fresh activity. Its nature, as well as its importance, are as yet hidden from us, but a stirring movement in the unconscious of many must be recognised and we must prepare ourselves for what is coming.

Mystics, saints, poets and artists have had, through the ages, a contact with undisclosed sources of energy with which, in this country, we are now learning to become familiar through dreams and their interpretations, and also through the practice of meditation – no longer for the few but for us all, the common people. The dispersal of the Buddhist monks from Tibet brought its teachers to Scotland. Zen has infiltrated from Japan, Vipassana from Thailand, Tao from China, Sufi teaching from the Near East, Trascendental Meditation, the Maharishi's teaching from India, now so widespread in America as well as in our own country and Europe.

For our day, it seems that these two disciplines, psychoanalysis and meditation, involving awareness of our breathing, are awakening to those who submit to their practice, deeply repressed feelings and memories of childhood, infancy, and even pre-natal conditions. The energy, formerly used in repression, is liberated and we must question how it is to be used, if not creatively then, all too probably, destructively. A clear analogy is in the use of electricity, which we find it hard to believe was scarcely in use to supply heat, light and power, until well into our present century. As lightning, electricity can bring death and disaster, but once this power was disciplined and controlled, it revolutionised life in the civilised world. It seems possible, even probable, that our spiritual energy likewise need no longer come fortuitously into our lives so that we designate it to chance or accident, but that it will find its channels in ways of which we are as yet unconscious.

Here and there among our neighbours and friends are some whom we say are 'live wires'. It is an interesting use of symbolism. How does a wire become alive – only a piece of metal with the capacity to stretch and lengthen, perhaps across the street, but also across the Atlantic? It is only when it is in contact with the source of electricity that it comes alive and carries the message. Power, not in the wire but channelled through it, creates miracles unknown even a century ago, and this is now outmoded by 'wireless', an even greater miracle. When the wire comes alive, then, very commonly, a light goes on to give us notice that it is in use. Let us look out for this light in the faces and attitudes of our 'live wire' friends when they are carrying news of available light and power into the experience of others, far and near.

Energy is intangible, invisible, but we recognise it by its ability to put things into action – 'to move mass', the physicists tell us. Solid masses of unbelief, of negativity, of anxiety and dread of the future are badly in need of the action which results when the energy of the psyche, or spirit, is liberated. What about the words – used so often glibly and unthinkingly – "Thine is the Kingdom the Power and the Glory." Do they speak to us of areas in our lives where light is breaking in on darkness, where energy is awaiting discovery of its potential, power not our own? Let us remember St. Paul's thanksgiving, "Glory be to Him whose power working in us" (that is when the wire becomes alive) "does infinitely more than we can ask or imagine."

(Appeared in *New Humanity*, 1982)

# Fidelity

In the later years of my life I have come to value the writing of St Paul. In the modern translations of his work, such as the Jerusalem Bible, we find him in contact with his converts from whom he was separated and unlikely to meet at all frequently, if ever again. To-day, I feel these letters are of great importance.

His teaching follows on the Logos wisdom of St. John's Gospel where the man Jesus, aware that he was at the point of physical death, saw clearly the meaning of the years he had lived as a man, not ashamed to call human beings his brothers, yet with complete clarity, aware that time would no longer have importance in life, but that, by dying, he was able to liberate, to set free, the spririt existing apart from time and space. He likened it to the sap of the vine, drawn from the earth through the roots, creating the branches which, as they received the flow of the sap, bore fruit; without the unity of branch and vine there can be no fruit. The abundant life in the vine gives an abundance of fruit.

St. Paul takes up the story of "Christ in us" and all his teaching emphasises this same message – "Christ in us", "Not I but Christ" "Christ Jesus is to us wisdom and virtue, holiness and freedom." "No longer I", he reiterates, but the indwelling spirit existing, out of time, out of space now with humanity for ever.

The word fidelity, or faithfulness, is one of the spiritual fruits listed by St. Paul, and is one about which there is great need on which to meditate today, when infidelity between husband and wife, with consequent inevitable infidelity to the children, seems to be rife in our society. Marriage is no longer thought of as a sacred bond, the wedding vows are all too often considered negligible.

At this point, I would like to take you to Zambia or, indeed, to any state in Africa uncontaminated by white civilisation. This is how, I am told, life develops for a small boy born into a primitive family in a village remote from western infiltration. For the first three years of his life, the babe lives in close contact with his mother's body, strapped to her back between her shoulders.

Wherever she goes, he goes with her, so that, in their own abode, or wherever her work takes her, there is no separation. From the age of three till he is seven, the child is part of the village community, accepted in neighbouring families, whether related by blood, or only be residential proximity. At seven, he is strong enough, and secure enough in himself, to be sent out to work, and becomes a herdsman, tending the cattle in the fields, aware of his own territory, and defending it against intrusion by his fellows. At fourteen, or thereabouts, when puberty asserts itself, he is sent into the house of a close relative, separated now from his mother, and here he is taught things that he needs to know about life in marriage and in community.

Then comes initiation when, after vigourous trials of his manhood, he is accepted as adult. Something more, however, has to happen before the tribe allows him to marry. *He must build a house and create a garden.* After all, the birds have set a good example, they build a nest before they lay their eggs and hatch their fledgelings. Bride and bridegroom must feel a renewal of the security they first experienced on their mothers' backs.

Security and anxiety to not exist side by side in our lives, one replaces the other, and I am assured that, in these primitive African communities, there is no anxiety neurosis afflicting the people. Only where civilisation demands education, the women go to college, and later to work, involving separation form their infants, do these tragic symptoms develop in the next generation.

Robert Ardrey's book, published some years ago, *The Territorial Imperative*, teaches us of the wisdom of Nature's set-up, where life-space is allocated for breeding and rearing, where offspring are secure, where invaders are fought off as unwelcome. Today, it may be we are learning again, if we heed our dreams and analyse them, that each of us has a right to this endowment of life-space. In the dream, it is likely to be symbolised by a house or castle courtyard, by a market square, a college quadrangle, a tennis court, a swimming bath, or other four-sided area. Jung has taught us to value them as life-space – the *Temenos*. It provides us and ours with security, and, in order to defend it, we come to maturity and develop the aggression which is a neccessity for survival.

Let us then see and understand that fidelity, faithfulness, has a dependence on material earthiness, as well as spritual and emotional values. The building of the houses establishes a home living-space for family and guests, whereby contact and close relationship, love and tenderness can develop. Remember how the poet, Robert Browning, has written "Not soul helps body more than body soul". We are psycho-physical beings dependent on both sides of our nature.

In broken homes, so deplorably common today, the family often lives in lodgings, in temporary accomodation, perhaps under the roof of in-laws, or even without a room they can call their own. We may hope that when the life of the spirit fills the lives of the growing-up people of today, they will have the patience and resources necessary to 'build a house and cultivate a garden', so that the life-space is prepared for what lies ahead between them.

All through the Old Testament Scriptures, God's faithfulness is noted and stressed and through it, we are encouraged to find our security, "He is faithful that promised". He made his covenant with Noah and renewed it through the ages. In the Christ today, we are involved in a new convenant through which our lives can be changed and bear the fruit of faithfulness.

What about the unfaithful people, whom we are meeting constantly from day-to-day at the present time? Can we find an answer through which their condition can be mended? We must all feel deeply pessimistic contemplating this condition of affairs, and yet, who are we to condemn them or to lose hope of better things? There is always an element of the miraculous in life, of a change in the hearts of mankind. Forces are working which we little understand but, by believing in them, we increase their energy, and ever more change becomes possible through enlightenment.

The capacity for fidelity to their fellows, I would point out, must, of necessity, develop in the individual and take over from the primitive self-interest, egocentricity. Much will depend on the early parent-child relationship. Rootedness in parental love, and space in which to grow, are essential for fruit-bearing. Let us take note again that fidelity, faithfulness, is one of the fruits of the spirit – only a good tree bears good fruit. The negative side of the picture is sad to contemplate, when, from one generation to another, the care and lovingness of the parents do not develop, fructify, come to life. It is important to be continually seeking and hoping to find ways in which love may be born again into the family situation. We believe that the will of God and the love of God are forever seeking their way into the lives of man, which gives us courage to maintain our hope that there will be a reversal in even the sad cases of deprived, unloved families.

I frequently stress the use of psychoanalysis in depth, and of meditation. Looking around us, we become conscious of much movement towards more spiritual development, bringing hope for new family attitudes, which will make the children secure. Each of us, perhaps, has some capacity to influence and to help young people as their lives open. Yet, here too, in this field we are glad to admit that beyond us, and above us, is a Spirit "other than our mortal own", a power making for righteousness, for fidelity, for the security of the individual, that is ever alive, ever moving, ever flowing with its purpose of integration and of bringing wholeness of life for each of us and for society at large.

(Appeared in *Science of Thought Review*, 1980)

Listen to the wind Nicodemus! Listen to the wind! You can hear it's sound, the night is full of it, hark to it in the tops of the trees – but where it has come from and where it is going no man knows. Now, Nicodemus, the Spirit of God is like that – invisible yet unmistakeable, unimpalpable yet full of power, able to do wonderful things for you if only you will stand in it's path and turn your face to it and open your life to it's influence. Just listen to the wind Nicodemus, listen to the wind.

# Physicians of the Psyche

Psychiatry today is at a cross-roads. Is it to work towards a condition known as normality? Let us think of normality as a level east and west highway across the land. Travelling on it, anxiety is at a minimum. We shall meet few risks or dangers. It will be deadly dull, but what matter! Turning off, however, to north or south, we shall meet ups and downs. Sometimes we will be confronted with 'Hill Difficulty', at other times, we will not know how deeply we have to drop, before the road again evens out and is easy.

Let us follow the main road and find ourselves in a psychiatric hospital with about twenty others committed to training in this branch of medicine. Roughly, we find that the students are divided into two batches of equal numbers. Most of them have recently emerged from medical school, having passed many examinations and seeing ahead more, leading to membership of the Royal College of Psychiatrists. If they study hard enough for the next few years, they will find themselves moving up a ladder – Junior Registrar, Senior Registrar, and now Consultant, with Medical Superintendent of a Psychiatric Hospital and a possible Professorship in the offing. Retirement at sixty-five will bring an assured pension and 'nothing to do'.

During these years, they will have read many text-books and been assiduous in keeping up with the journals, and many patients will have passed through their hands. These patients will have had, in each case, a preliminary diagnostic interview on admission – if the person is sane enough to give them a rational account of his illness. 'At last', he says, 'someone is interested and will listen to my story.' The trainee psychiatrist learns to take as adequate a history as can be made in the allotted time, and he leaves the patient hopeful with the assurance that they will be seeing each other again. If an hour or two is allocated to the diagnosic interview, the authorities tend to discourage any further similar session. "Fifteen minutes weekly is sufficient for you to give to any one patient." Here I quote an actual instruction given by a Medical Superintendent to a trainee within the last twelve months. It is good, however, to realise that there are hospitals in which more time is being allocated to the listening process.

The diagnosis is considered to be of great importance. Textbooks gave the main part of their content to this until quite recently. In first and early editions of the standard text book, 'Henderson and Gillespie', treatment was hardly mentioned. The padded cell had gone out of fashion, but the drugs which control the emotions were slow to appear – sodium and potassium bromides and the foul-tasting paraldehyde (used mainly in emergency) were the sedatives to calm the overactive psyche, until matters began to change during the 1914–18 war. Luminal and Trional were very 'new-fangled' and were not in common use until after the war had finished. I recollect getting free samples of these drugs from Switzerland, I think probably in early 1914, and that they were not available once the war had started, but were widely used as hyponotics in the years following. Miltown, a tranquilliser, the first to be given that hopeful name, crept across the Atlantic, but was in scarce supply in the latter years of Hitler's war. Then there was a great explosion of drug activity with Pheno-barbitone and later with its many successors coming on to the therapeutic scene.

Shock-therapy was introduced from Italy at the end of the second World War and very great hope was aroused that manic-depressive illness had come under control. Undoubtedly, in some cases it seemed to have a lasting benefit, but all too soon it had to be recognised that not only were the results often of short duration but also that serious loss of memory might be permanent. It is sad to think how inhumanely this method could be used. A patient whom I had in my charge twenty years ago had been given two hundred shocks for a postnatal depression occurring after her first child was born. As a result, she completely lost the memory of courtship, engagement, marriage and the months of pregnancy – a devastating loss. With a second child conceived and born in spite of many warnings against, and much intimidation by the powers that be, there was only slight temporary depression, and the child has developed a real genius as a musician. The world would have lost much had her courage not overcome the advice of important people.

We should not underestimate the importance of these mood-changing drugs – anti-depressants, anti-psychotics, anti-schizo-phrenics, and suchlike. Their use with patients affected has given rise to a huge pharmaceutical industry with widespread distribution and availability. Whereas it would be foolish to deny their usefulness when used discreetly, it is also necessary to observe how their use quite commonly leads to addiction.

Electric shock therapy is still widely used as an alternative to drugs but insulin shock therapy, at one time very popular, has now been almost completely discarded as of value in treatment.

To return to our trainee psychiatrists who, having been trained in diagnosis, are now battling with pharmacology and treatment – and the treatment of the diagnosed conditions by a vast array of drugs. Family doctors no longer need to send their patients to the hospital if anxiety is the main symptom. Largactil and valium have largely ousted pheno-barbitone from the general practitioner's prescription pad. Whether these drugs are prescribed by hospital doctors or in general practice, there is a recommendation that their administration should be continued indefinitely – presumably for the rest of the patient's lifetime. The results of withdrawal are often very serious and we come to the sad conclusion that the hospital and other physicians are creating drug addicts at an alarming rate with, incidentally, enormous drug bills for which the taxpayer is responsible.

What is happening to the trainees? They have sorted themselves out in to two lots; in one group we find the idealists who entered the psychiatric wards with genuine desire to lessen the suffering of patients and their relatives in the grip of schizophrenia, manic depression, obsessions, and such states. Disillusionment with what is happening disquiets them profoundly and many escape to take up general practice or one of the other specialities, skins, eyes, etc. The others, the second group, find themselves landed in psychiatry and, although disillusioned, they have not the courage to break away. They have, perhaps, entered psychiatry because they are insufficiently sure of themselves to do clinical work, except in a hospital or other institution where responsibility would not lie too heavily on their shoulders. Immaturity and anxiety do not make a good background for those who set out to rescue others from their psychological distresses.

Today, then, let us look again at this problem of discovering adequate staff to man the hospitals of the future, where something more than drug addiction and shock-therapy need to be brought to bear on the problems of those seeking guidance and healing in their affliction. "Physician, know thyself" is a behest that psychoanalysis has made possible during the current century. All too often, the role of the physician is adopted by men and women with a very scanty appreciation of what is involved in commitment to the profession. Their motives for becoming a doctor may be compulsive and not by any means clear to themselves. I have, for instance, had patients who, as children, had been committed to hospital life for a prolonged period and had, in consequence, an identification with 'the chief', the doctor in charge of the ward. Their pathetic attempts to qualify or, if able to pass the necessary examinations, to undertake the responsibility required, and to develop the caring personality without which medical work can be sterile, have never been fulfilled.

Dr. John Bowlby and his colleagues have shown how damaging prolonged separation from the parents may be to a child in hospital, blocking his capacity for feeling. Other environmental factors may have been at work affecting the capacity of those who offer themselves for membership of the psychiatric profession – not easy to notice at early interviews, but likely to hinder their development as adequate therapists in the profession. The value of psychoanalysis is still a matter of controversy, and methods of treatment still lie open to criticism and even suspicion.

At this point, I would like to contribute what I believe to be fundamental decisions that we, as the more experienced staff of the Davidson Clinic, made in considering who should be admitted to the rank of analyst, or, at least, trained with this in view. To begin with, I may say that we had very many doctors and others coming to us in the twenty-five years of our existence, asking to be trained as analysts. I must emphasise that our Clinic stood solidly and relentlessly for analysis, by which was understood the exploration of the unconscious by dream interpretation. Conscious methods of treatment and the giving of advice were not acceptable. Freud's statement that the dream is the royal road to the unconscious was honoured, but, from the early days, Jungian, as well as Freudian interpretations were considered acceptable. Neither school in its orthodoxy accepted our work. Groddeck's teaching was a leavening factor, and psychosomatic illness was recognised and willingly treated. Perhaps the most important aspect of the faithful, patient, analytic clinic enterprise was the emergence of creative potential. There was an element of the unexpected about this or, perhaps, we had not been told to expect it. We found that analysis, if faithfully carried out by the analyst and the patient (analysand), inevitably bore fruit which was obvious. Certainly, relationships became easier, husband-wife, parent-child, teacher and pupils, employer and his workers – even siblings could report less jealousy, more friendship. Hidden gifts, such as unused talents in music, painting and design, drama, poetry, descriptive writing, and teaching, in all these and in other ways – perhaps barely noticed – something was happening, the gifts were being used creatively. Can you realise how rewarding this was, and always will be, in the analytic situation, which is by no means always either easy or pleasant?

I have said that even in the early days of the Davidson Clinic, people came wanting to beome analysts. Here, "Physician know thyself" was an inexorable condition, so we would urge them to undertake their own personal analysis and, in due time, we and they would be able to decide on their suitability. One of our oft-repeated statements in this connection was that it takes five years to make a plumber. In those days the apprenticeship was all-important, and could not be omitted or hurried. Many could not stay the course, they analysed their motives for their ambition, and quitted. Those who submitted to the long apprenticeship, continuing their own analytic sessions, were, in due time, given patients with whom they worked under supervision, and encouraged to undertake the patients' analysis by listening to their dreams, allowing feeling to bring empathy, and learning the discipline of avoiding giving advice. Here, too, creativity of hidden gifts, intuitive wisdom lying dormant, is brought into the service of others. The patients are awakened to discover their own centre, the Self, through which contact with deeper spiritual energy is established, and they find increasingly, and more surely, the open way of life.

Returning again to the trainees in psychiatric hospitals, their number now reduced by the flight of their fellows into other fields, as a result of disillusionment with inadequate methods of treatment. Here we come to face the crucial question of how to make the best of these young men and women asking to be trained as physicians of the psyche and to learn to deal with the problems of the crippled, ineffective people presenting themselves for treatment and with hope of healing.

What is it that really matters in the personality of this man or woman, who now is ready to pass into the ranks of the psychiatric profession, ready to be accounted *psyche-iatros*, physician of the psyche? Has he developed, and is he able to use his full potential as a human being, since the work he sets himself to undertake in the healing of the sick will demand of him not only knowledge of disordered minds, but much more.

A question that once seemed important in the diagnostic interview – 'Is there insanity in the family?' – might well be replaced by asking whether parents, grandparents, and others connected with his infancy, had any capacity for loving care, any capacity for tender warm contact – perhaps simplified into the question – 'Do you remember being cuddled as a child?'

Does this psychiatrist, on the threshold of his career, remember being cuddled as a child? (What a question! Really, how can you be so naive?) Surely, however, it is legitimate to enquire as to whether he has warmth of feeling, ability to assess the suffering of his patients and their relatives, who need this service if he is to be an instrument of healing.

If deprived of it in infancy, it is still possible, through the relationship (transference) created in analysis, that this feeling will emerge in him and be available for his work. All too often scholastic requirements over-estimate the work of the mind, the intellect, the learning, at the expense of the heart, with its capacity for love and feeling.

In the year 1912, a terrible disaster occurred in the Atlantic Ocean – a great ship, the Titanic, collided with an iceberg, and was lost with many on board. Had the iceberg consisted only of the obvious area which could be seen above the surface, little harm would have been done. Under the surface of the ocean, however, lay a great mass, immeasurably greater than the visible peak, and it was upon this concealed mass that the great ship was destroyed.

Let us look at the symbolism of what happened that April day, interpreting it as if it were a dream. Before, however, we build up the picture and give it a meaning, let us see the ocean as that out of which emerges everything as we know it in our world today, the rocks, the sand, the salts crystallising, reflecting light, bringing colour. Then life appears, the algae, the seaweeds, the protozoa, sponges, living things not yet clearly defined as vegetable or animal. The tree of life has its roots in the ocean. The growth is dependent on water; even human life has its own small ocean for the first two hundred and eighty days of its life. Scientists assure us that the ocean flows in our blood vessels.

What can we make of the iceberg – how interpret its existence in the ocean? Sea-water was become structured. Is then, the iceberg a symbol of the psyche, only the superficial aspects of which come into consciousness? Are the visible peaks symbols of individuals, island-like to outer view, but all part of an immense mass concealed in the ocean? Can this underwater mass symbolise the unity of all psychic existence? Can we best conceive of humanity as one? Do all inter-relate in one? A human physical body contains millions of cells, comparable, maybe, to the number of human beings in the world today.

The great oceans are full of life, some static, as the sea vegetation, but also the whales and dolphins, the fishes innumerable, also the protozoa and the coral organisms. No limit can be placed on the ocean, nor can we, going beneath the surface, define the limits of the human unconscious. What about 'the Glory that shall be revealed' and the glimpse that the early poets, who composed the Psalms, had of what lies beyond man's awareness?

As the days pass, there will be clarification of this idea that, in the deep unconscious of humanity, there is constant interchange and flow in life's happenings, affecting us all as individuals, yet united at the deepest level. Chance, which we mention so lightly as if it explained a coming together of events, may rather come to be understood as strands in a great web of being.

As Francis Thompson has so beautifully written:

> "All things by immortal power
> Near or far,
> Hiddenly
> To each other linkèd are,
> That thou canst not stir a flower
> Without troubling of a star".

(from 'The Mistress of Vision'.)

(*1982*)

# Peace

The lectures have dealt with conflict as it affects man's psyche – conflict in the infant, in groups, in families and between nations. We have been asked to tolerate conflict in children and not increase their difficulties and add to their guilt by punishing them. We have been urged to meet in groups and talk so that the causes of these inner strains may come to the surface. We have been shown how war has a positive, as well as negative, value just as in all life there is the rhythm of breaking down and of building again. Arnold Toynbee in his study of history points to the origin of our solar system, and therefore to the origin of life as we know it, in a destructive phase when another star came near to hitting the sun and so caused the planets to be thrown off course. In the terminology of the Chinese, the Yin phase of perfection was succeeded by the Yang phase of destruction, and in this moment Creation took place.

Peace, then, may be sterile or creative. The babe in the womb is at peace cut off from all relationship but one, safe, secure, no harm can befall him, but he is sterile in his isolation. To be born is to be related and once born we cannot escape relationship, mother, father – the family, the milkman, the postman, people in the street, the school, the factory, the office, the world. Now to live in relationship involves conflict. The young baby may avoid it for a time if he is much wanted and much loved. We call this the pre-ambivalent stage of infancy. Inevitably, and all too soon, the two-sideness of life becomes apparent, love and hate, desire and fear, conflict is observable, war is declared.

Where can we begin if Peace is to come in our time? There are some possible answers.

(1) Begin with the mothers. Help them by our sympathy and encouragement to be utterly loving, patient, full of understanding, slow to punish and frustrate their children. But there are such things as shopping queues, washing-days, full buses. Sooner or later come impatience, threats, slaps, with the children in tears and

afraid. Still, to begin with the mothers is a good idea. We can help them to understand, to be less likely to punish, more willing to find other ways, to avoid unnecessary conflict, to be jolly and laugh sometimes instead of scolding, to give more freedom and encourage their children to find their own right way. Fathers too may be helped to give up sergeant-major patterns learned perhaps in the army or from their own fathers.

(2) We may begin with the children themselves. Let them play both constructively and destructively. Give each child confidence in at least one grown-up who will love and tolerate them whether good or bad. Encourage their self-respect and allow them to develop initiative through allowing them freedom.

(3) Dr Frank Freemont Smith who came from America to help with the organisation of Mental Health in this country said he thought we might begin with two groups, the *nursery school teachers* and the *diplomats*. Encourage these people to have psychological analysis and a good start would be made in making a more peaceful world.

(4) In the Davidson Clinic we are glad to think that we can begin with our patients, and we have very great happiness when they testify that their homes are much more peaceful places since they entered the way of understanding through psychological treatment.

(5) Now for the real truth, the secret which has evaded us so often. The only *place* where we *can* begin is with ourselves – you with yourself, I with myself. The only *time* in which we can begin is now. Yesterday is past and to-morrow never comes, *now* is the creative moment. So then the next question must be – What can we do about ourselves now? The answer is 'Seek for awareness'. Awareness of what? I can suggest a few of many answers:

(a) Be aware of our motives. They are recognisable under the demanding phrase 'I want'. I want food and drink, knowledge, power, love, children, fulfilment along many ways. It is not beyond our capacity to analyse our motives to some extent at least. Awareness involves neither condemnation nor condonation.

(b) Be aware of our projections. Recently driving my car I came to a three-way corner. Ahead of me in a shop window I saw a car approaching, its lamps alight although it was daytime. "How foolish some people are," I thought, but a moment later I had to ask "Can it be me?" as indeed it was. This question must often be asked 'Can it be me?' Sometimes at least the answer is 'Yes'.

(c) Awareness of our masks too is necessary. Each of us dresses up to impress the world – each of us has a secret personality we keep hidden, or think we do. A patient at the Davidson Clinic used to meet me on the stair and came to the conclusion that I was bad-tempered and arrogant. When his analyst told me of this I said "How strange, I have always spoken to him in a friendly way". "Yes" was the answer. "He is more aware than you of your-shadow, your inner self." Whenever we see 'unsuccessful' photographs or catch an unexpected glimpse of ourselves in a mir-ror we know what we look like when we discard the mask. Notice please that we cannot straight away discard our masks in society, but it is good that we should be aware of them.

(d) Awareness is a still more creative attitude when we become aware of the creative and purposeful nature of psychic energy in our lives – we may call it awareness of the Will and the Purpose of God.

All this awareness is a distinctively human capacity and it is pro-bable that it is emergent in evolution. Men to-day are thought, for instance, to be conscious of a wider range of colours than in Homeric times. When unconscious conflicts come into awareness, that is into consciousnesss, then it is possible to deal with them by means of other human attributes – namely intelligence, love and humour. The animals, even those near to us in evolution, or close to us through domestication, show only gleams of intelligence and humour. Love in the animal world is almost wholly confined to mother-instinct, and the love of a creature for its master. In man it is a widespread altruism. It is doubtful if any animal laughs, but all humans do, through not always very long or very loud.

To recapitulate:

1. Peace is not what happens when people stop fighting.
2. Peace may be sterile, achieved by giving up relationship and liv-ing in isolation.
3. Creative peace is achieved through relationship and through the human aspects of relationship understanding, love and humour.

(*Final lecture in series "Why War? A Psychological Approach," Autumn 1948*)

# Flag Day

## The Clinic in Contact with the Man in the Street

Flag Day is primarily thought of as a means of raising funds, and this indeed is an important aspect of what happens that day.

There are others, however, of which I would like to write while the impact of this day is upon us. One of these is the contact which we obtain with Edinburgh people. This year we had seven kiosks, most of them situated in Princes Street. In each of these one member of the Staff was in charge, with a bevy of collectors who brought in their full tins and carried away others to fill, with fresh supplies of flags, and receiving words of appreciation and encouragement.

I suppose quite ninety per cent of the passers-by put in their coppers, their sixpences or shillings just as a levy, 'another flag day', and in a certain sense this is what we aim at receiving – people don't miss the small sums contributed. 'Mony a mickle maks a muckle', and the heavy load of coppers is converted into many pounds sterling. The other ten per cent are people who stop and make some remark, some question is asked about the purpose of the Clinic; someone may say, "Yes, that's a good cause". Occasionally "I don't approve" or "I wouldn't contribute to *that*" we were encouraged to find how many people do know and responded generously, the half-crowns and paper money were tokens of gratitude and sympathy.

The disapprovers varied – some "on principle" that psychiatry is a bad thing, that psychoanalysis is useless, that all this sort of thing could be avoided if parents beat their children more systematically, that experts were not needed – "I can do this work as well as anyone though I don't set up as a psychiatrist." That it is only stupid people who have "nerves", folk should learn to pull themselves together and so on.

The question "What is it all about, the work of this Clinic?"

could not be very quickly answered. We had some papers and pamphlets to hand out, but often there was no time. I found myself saying "It's for people in trouble, troublesome children, troublesome parents, troublesome husbands, troublesome wives, troublesome bosses," – but by that time, fortunately, there would be more flags wanted or the questioner would find he was in a hurry. Sometimes there were specific complaints, "It's the head doctor I don't like". As Honorary Medical Director I had to dodge this one and was glad I was not recognised as such. The fact that we charge fees was brought up against us and one gentleman said "Na, Na, I would not contribute to a Tory organisation". We wonder whether he has a Tory inside him whom he is ready to project on to anything.

The second point I would like to make is that all the friends who organised and worked so devotedly to make the day a success, and the many conveners and collectors, were doing more than taking in cash. They were bringing their energy, both physical and spiritual energy, into the heart of the Clinic. As Medical Director I felt personal gratitude to each and all, many old and trusted friends, others who scarcely knew anything of our work but who by their co-operation gave us strength and support.

It is sometimes difficult to beg either for money or for services, but more difficult in anticipation than in the here and now. "I am enjoying myself" was often repeated on Saturday as the heavy tins were brought back to our welcoming hands. "It's good fun" – and so the money came in. Toll was taken from the Edinburgh public to a total of £939, but also a two-way impact was made through which again many things we hope will begin to happen.

(*The Bulletin, October 1950*)

# Radio Four Interview by Leslie Smith

*Preamble*: Winifred Rushforth graduated in medicine at Edinburgh University in 1908. During the 72 years since she has practised variously as a physician, gynaecologist and surgeon but eventually she took up psychiatry, and for over fifty years now that has been her calling. Her interest in psychology was stimulated by Freud's writings though not actually started by them. Long before she had even heard of Freud she was fascinated by what she called 'the inner workings of the mind'. Eventually she came into contact with some of the other pioneers in the field of psychology, including Adler. She heard him lecture and she met him, and she came to know Jung personally too. I met Winifred Rushforth last autumn shortly after she had celebrated another birthday at her Edinburgh home, where with just a little domestic help several times a week she lives entirely on her own.

*Smith*: Are you still working with patients?

*Rushforth*: I am working with individual patients doing psychoanalysis, seeing perhaps four of five patients a day. Then I have a group every night and sometimes groups in the day too.

*Smith*: So really you are working full time.

*Rushforth*: I am working just about as hard as ever I have in my life.

*Smith*: Although you are now aged...

*Rushforth*: 94!

*Smith*: It is very hard to believe that!

*Rushforth*: It is hard for me to believe it sometimes. I don't feel very different from what I did when I was perhaps 21; tired a bit sometimes.

*Smith*: Though not too tired to accept invitations to lecture to various university and other groups in widely scattered parts of Scotland. At what stage of your early life did you first think of a medical career?

*Rushforth*: I think very very early on. It is associated with my nurse. I was very fortunate in having a nurse who was a South African woman, a coloured woman. How she landed up in Scotland is another story, but she came into our household before I was born and she took me over and..she always called me 'my girlie'. She was a nannie and we called her 'Nursie' and she and I had a great deal of communication. I asked her endless questions of course and when I said to her one day 'how does the wax get into my ear, Nursie', she said, 'oh you must ask your Aunt, she will know, she is a doctor.

*Smith*: Ah, so there was a tradition of medicine in the family.

*Rushforth*: Very much so. My father's sister was one of the very first women doctors. She graduated as a doctor in 1880 before I was born.

*Smith*: That must actually have been just about the first ever.

*Rushforth*: She was the tenth woman on the General Medical Register – a real pioneer. I had always wanted to be a doctor; I think my motivation was curiosity, I had wanted to know, to understand: where do babies come from?; nobody would tell me. No. no, no, that was a trade secret, 'you'll know soon enough'.

*Smith*: But in the days when you were a medical student was there still not the idea that this was a man's job rather than a woman's?

*Rushforth*: Very much so, in fact unspoken or sometimes spoken, because I had a brother who was a medical student, 'what cheek you have thinking you can be a doctor'!

*Smith*: When you qualifed what did you do next?

*Rushforth*: I went to Dundee as an assistant in general practice. There was a woman there who had been a doctor in general practice for sixteen years. I thought, what a long time to be a doctor. Now I have been a doctor as you see for over seventy years but it seemed to me then that she was getting on, perhaps coming to the end of her usefulness!

*Smith*: For a young woman at that time, just after the turn of the century, presumably it was regarded as faintly indecent to have a professional ambition rather than to wish to get married and settle down.

*Rushforth*: I don't know if I would say that. There were even women graduating in law and certainly there were a great many women taking arts degrees.

*Smith*: Presumably you hoped to have a happy married life and a family rather than to go on working?

*Rushforth*: I never thought of giving up working, nor did I ever give up my work. My husband was good to me, he allowed himself to share me with my profession.

*Smith*: How did you meet your husband?

*Rushforth*: I met him in India; I had gone out to a mission hospital and he came out as a young government servant a year later.

*Smith*: Was this after you had done your postgraduate year in Dundee?

*Rushforth*: Yes.

*Smith*: Why did you go to India?

*Rushforth*: Although I said my motive in becoming a doctor was curiosity, wanting to *know*, I think that I always wanted to be involved with caring. In India at that time the purdah system for women was still operating and they could not get any attention except through women. Quite early in my student career I came in contact with people who were going out as missionaries – I think even before that probably I had intended to go out to India, or to Africa as my nurse was an African.

*Smith*: Did you have any wish to do good, was it a kind of virtuous feeling that led you to become a missionary doctor?

*Rushforth*: It is very difficult to separate that from one's other feelings. Other people point a finger at you and say 'oh, you're a do gooder', but what would we do without the do-gooders?!

*Smith*: And did you do good?

*Rushforth*: Well I often look back on it rather laughing at myself because I think I had a very good time in India during those five years as a mission doctor. I began to understand something of the Indian people, although rather regretfully not perhaps in enough depth, but I made a great many friends and I had a good time.

*Smith*: And you met your husband there?

*Rushforth*: Yes, we were engaged for quite a long time while he was in the Indian Finance Service. He was a mathematician and musician and a very gifted and sensitive man. It is a very very interesting thing, isn't it, this falling in love. I have just been writing about it in my book. Who has the capacity to fall in love? What is it? It is partly physical isn't it, but unless it is also spiritual it is unsatisfactory.

*Smith*: What do you mean by spiritual?

*Rushforth*: Well we are psyche, we have bodies, and there is that which the spirit can meet, something more than just bodily proximity. There is the coming together of the things of the mind and of the spirit.

*Smith*: And so you fell in love with each other?

*Rushforth*: Very much so, yes. Fortunately I know that.

*Smith*: How do you know that?

*Rushforth*: Well we tested it out for thirty years and we kept on caring for each other during that time.

*Smith*: You had thirty years of married life?

*Rushforth*: Yes.

*Smith*: And you had how many children?

*Rushforth*: Four children, two girls and then two boys, but I had to be partly separated from them. The tragedy of life in India, at that time was that it was considered wrong to keep one's children in the hot climate. Nowadays they do it more I think.

*Smith*: So in a way there were three separations in your life. The children who were away from you in this country, that is to say far far away, your married life with your husband, and also your professional life – you had three partitions in a way.

*Rushforth*: Of course, yes.

*Smith*: Wasn't that rather unsatisfactory?

*Rushforth*: If it had meant a splitting of my personality it would have been a very tragic thing, but I think to the extent that I was able to hold the three aspects together it was an enriching thing.

*Smith*: Were you in fact able to embrace all three at once?

*Rushforth*: I think so, yes.

*Smith*: Why did you leave India?

*Rushforth*: We left India at the time of what we call the Wall Street Crisis, the Depression.

*Smith*: And so you came back to Scotland?

*Rushforth*: Yes, we were able to re-join the children and make the family life again.

*Smith*: And so when you came back to Scotland did you continue in General Practice?

*Rushforth*: No, I never went back to General Practice. I had given that up. This is when I got in touch with the Tavistock Clinic.

*Smith*: This is a good fifty years ago now?

*Rushforth*: Yes, I was at the Tavistock Clinic in 1929.

*Smith*: Why did you go there?

*Rushforth*: I had always wanted to know more about the inner things of life. I can remember as a school girl reading Virgil and when we came to the episode at Delphi when the Sybil said 'know thyself', I can remember now the sort of inner thrill that came to me, is there a way of knowing oneself? And it is interesting because that has always kept with me. A great many years later out in India, my eldest child I remember was in my arms at the time, a young woman friend had come out from London and she had a book which I now think must have been *The Psychopathology of Everyday Life*. I got very excited about the description of analysis, but this man Freud was in Vienna and undoubtedly he talked German – was my German adequate? I was in India, how could I ever get back? No, no, no, analysis was a thing I needn't dream about, but I had this same thrill over 'know thyself'. There is a bit of oneself that is unkown, unconscious – some way we must get in touch with it.

*Smith*: Of course to the general run of the public at that time and indeed for many people still Freud is a kind of – well I could say fraud – a man apparently obsessed with sex.

*Rushforth*: He was much more than obsessed with sex, his message was that he was obsessed with the unconscious, this unconscious motivation, the why, why, why, of life. Why do we do certain things, why do we say certain things, can we choose? I overlapped Freud's professional life by perhaps fifteen years I think, and I overlapped Jung's life. I knew Jung a bit. I heard him speak on various occasions, and I once had an hour with him in Zurich.

*Smith*: Did you correspond?

*Rushforth*: I can't tell you what I wrote about but I have this letter from him. "Thank you for your letter which has interested me very much indeed. It was with great pleasure that I read the account of your activities in your psycho-therapeutic clinic in Edinburgh. I send my greetings to you and your co-workers and all good wishes for the continued success of your undertaking. It is of great satisfaction to me to know (I like this bit) that this work I have started is continued beyond the present moment into a time which is no longer mine. Sincerely yours, C. G. Jung." It is very surprising how people do come here from what we say in Scotland, all the airts, all the different parts of the world. People from America. . .

*Smith*: Patients you mean are they?

*Rushforth*: Not necessarily, just people who say 'I am interested, I have heard about you.' A very comical thing happened recently which perhaps I can tell you: at 2 a.m. I was wakened by the telephone some months ago and I thought, who on earth is calling me at 2 a.m., and I discovered it was a call from Canada, Montreal, and I couldn't get the person to say who she was. I said how do you know about me? 'Many people have told me'. How did you know my telephone number? Again, many people have told me, which must have been a fib! 'I want you to pray for me, you always say that God is our Father, I want you to pray for me'! She continued for ten minutes, which must have cost her a lot because to communicate from Canada to Edinburgh costs a pound a minute, but she just evidently needed to be in touch with me and to this day I don't know who she was.

*Smith*: How important is religious belief in your life?

*Rushforth*: Very important indeed. I began my life with Nursie who taught me to pray for Africa which she called 'The Dark Country' and the people who lived there. As I went to a mission hospital we also had a religious background to our life there.

*Smith*: Would you say that your faith has strengthened or weakened over the years?

*Rushforth*: Very much strengthened. You cannot work with the psyche, without, I think, some growth of awareness of spiritual matters. The psyche and the spirit are not separate things.

*Smith*: When you say spiritual matters are you in fact meaning God?

*Rushforth*: Is God the ultimate reality? Yes I do mean God but we don't always talk about God, sometimes we have to avoid that.

*Smith*: Are you a churchgoer?

*Rushforth*: Not very much. I am a church member, and my Minister comes to see me sometimes. In the last two years I have been somewhat incapacited, I have a certain lack of mobility, but he forgives me for not going to church.

*Smith*: Who, the minister or God?

*Rushforth*: Both!

*Smith*: Do you believe in prayer?

*Rushforth*: Yes, every Sunday night I have a group of people, sometimes only six, sometimes up to a dozen who have been coming regularly for seven years, and we really keep this attitude of seeking for God. We use a translation of the Bible called The Jerusalem Bible which I feel sheds great light on the Scriptures. One of the things that happens in our Sunday night group is that we always begin by making the circle, by holding hands and repeating the Lord's Prayer. But before we say it, I say 'Lord, teach us to pray'. Now I have various people coming on Sunday night who have perhaps been churchgoers, and they say to me, 'we've been saying the Lord's Prayer all our lives but we are learning now to pray the Lord's Prayer'. That is what is happening to me too as I use the Lord's Prayer as a part of my meditation day by day. I suppose really in the last ten years, and it is interesting, you see, one doesn't need so much sleep in old age, and when I waken in the night it is then that I find that meditation is possible, indeed even easy.

*Smith*: How closely do you keep in touch with professional medical colleagues, and also with contemporary medicine?

*Rushforth*: Well some of my patients are doctors – I have at present two psychiatrists who come for analysis. I have always had colleagues amongst my patients and of course I value them very much indeed. They also come to realise, as everyone does in analysis, the importance of the more than physical, the importance of the unconscious; and ultimately of course we must say that God speaks to mankind through the unconscious, that the unconscious is the source of so much in our lives, of our energy. So the religious side is integral in my work, but sometimes I am asked not to talk about God – in fact fairly frequently people say 'please don't talk to me about God! I remember a professor who came to me and he said 'I can switch off the radio when the religious programmes come on and I will stop speaking to you if you get onto that line'. And then one day I found myself saying 'I am so sorry, I am afraid I am talking about God' and he said 'get on with it , I can take it now'!

*Smith*: You must of course be very aware that psychiatry is almost a dirty word now in many circles. People tend either to blame it for all the ills of the world or alternatively to say that it is really just a form of trickery, a kind of con.

*Rushforth*: Well I don't think that it is either of those, but I think that the psychiatrist is the physician of the psyche. I once had the honour of going to Buckingham Palace and I was told just that I would have the moment with the Queen, and she could either talk with me or I could just get my medal stuck on my bosom. The Queen said to me, 'And what is you speciality in medicine?', and I replied 'I am a psychiatrist'. 'Oh' she said, and passed me on!

*Smith*: What did you make of that?

*Rushforth*: I was so sorry that I hadn't taken the opportunity to say 'I am a physician of the psyche and would like to tell you a little more about it'!

*Smith*: Why were you at Buckingham Palace?

*Rushforth*: I got the O.B.E.

*Smith*: What for?

*Rushforth*: For my work in the Davidson Clinic here in Edinburgh which ran for 25 years.

*Smith*: What effect did the death of your husband have on you?

*Rushforth*: I think it opened up, rather than closed up my life. I still dream of him, very vividly and almost amusingly sometimes, because he is quite often scolding me. He is quite often telling me to get back to work, to get on with things!

*Smith*: You speak of opening up rather than of sorrow.

*Rushforth*: Yes, very definitely. A friend of my husband's who was at his Cremation Service said to me afterwards, 'your husband was with us in that service and it was triumphant' and he said 'I have always hated those Crematorium Services and have come away profoundly depressed, but I am not afraid of death any longer'. This man died within about a year himself and I was so glad that he had had that experience. My husband did live more than in the body I am quite sure.

*Smith*: Who would you say has influenced you most throughout your life, or during your life?

*Rushforth*: Well I suppose my husband really, and my own family. In my old age I quite often find myself thinking back to the beginnings of my life, to the nurse and the parents, and also my own patients. One of my rules is that if a patient doesn't get on well with analysis, I take them back to the parent of the opposite sex and in a curious way, really quite recently, I seem to have been saying to myself 'what about your father, what about your father, what was his influence about you?', and I see that this man, my father, was a cultured man; he was a farmer and he had been a student at Edinburgh University. He was an acquaintance of Robert Louis Stevenson. His people away back, really for centuries, had been farming people and their name was Bartholomew. It was an old Huguenot name and he used to tell me that my mother's name, Findlater, was also a Huguenot name. So it is possible that I am of Huguenot stock on both sides which I think is very fortunate. When you ask that question, what is the most important thing in your life, possibly just that inheritance.

*Smith*: Rather than any particular event, there must have been some events which have had a tremendous influence.

*Rushforth*: Yes many events – perhaps the day I started medicine. Perhaps the day I was married or the day I fell in love, as you say. Or the day my first child was born. We all come to crises in our lives, don't we; days when our horizons suddenly lift and we see further afield.

*Smith*: You mention the positive, the joyous occasions rather than any unhappy ones.

*Rushforth*: Very strangely I have been a happy woman all my life. I have of course had suffering, but it disappears into the blue and I don't focus on it, I focus on the fact that my life has been one of extreme fulfilment and happiness.

*Smith*: And is still?

*Rushforth*: Yes I am a very happy woman nowadays, it is very good for me to have so many friends and so many patients.

*Smith*: Do you ever contemplate retiring?

*Rushforth*: I have contemplated it. I did retire. In fact I retired several times; the last time I retired was when I had an illness two years ago and. . .

*Smith*: This was when you were already in your nineties?

*Rushforth*: Yes I was ninety-two and I had – really instead of walking steadfastly, nowadays I stagger somewhat – as I tell my friends it is not either the pleasure or the expense of alcohol. But I had been off work for a couple of months and I thought, well it is time I retired. At 92 I have done enough – this is the end of it. But when I got back here I opened a letter and it said 'Dear Dr. Rushforth, 19 years ago I was your patient, you helped me as nobody had ever helped me since, can I come back and see you?' And I went to the phone and said, 'come tomorrow' and that was the end of my retirement!

*Smith*: So you have been in practice again ever since! Would you like to retire?

*Rushforth*: Not now. I suppose I will die one of these days. . .

*Smith*: How long would you like to live?

*Rushforth*: I had a very curious dream in which I saw chalked up very clearly 'Dr. Winifred Rushforth 102'.

*Smith*: Well that is a good seven or eight years.

*Rushforth*: Well that comforts my patients and they say 'it's alright Doc, don't worry, we can come to you for a bit yet'. I suppose my life has been divided into those three epochs, one might almost call them – I was thirty years old when I married and I was sixty years old when my husband died. From that time, it is another thirty-four years, each of those periods has been different in a way, markedly different, but each with its own fulfilment.

*Smith*: How important are your family to you and your grandchildren?

*Rushforth*: They are very very very important and dear to me. I have very good relationships, especially with those grandchildren who are now in their twenties. They come back to me. They all call me Winifred, I am not Granny, I might be Winifred Granny of Granny Winifred, but they are very close to me; they write to me, they come to see me, they share a great deal with me. I feel very very very thankful for them.

*Smith*: Any great grandhildren?

*Rushforth*: I have eight, yes. Four girls and four boys, but I have – I am a matriarch, you see, and I suppose I am proud to be a matriarch.

*Smith*: What do you mean by a matriarch?

*Rushforth*: I am a mother of more than just my own children. Even a woman who has no children may be the mother of thousands and it is very curious to me that although I have – I was counting it up the other day, about twenty descendents, counting my own children and grandchildren and greatgrandchildren, but I must have hundreds of people who have been with me for periods – some of them only a few days some of them for many years.

*Smith*: As patients you mean?

*Rushforth*: As patients or just as visitors. Even this morning I had a packet from Australia and I couldn't think who it had come from. I felt I knew nobody in Australia and then I remembered a particular man who had come to this room, I suppose perhaps three years ago, and I had forgotten all about him. That is the sort of thing that happens, they come, they perhaps sit here for a few hours and they go away again.

*Smith*: Do you like children?

*Rushforth*: Yes, very much. I am very very pleased to have great grandchildren and they are very bonny and sweet and interesting. It is lovely to me to see the next generation coming on and to think that each generation perhaps just now has a better opportunity than the last.

*Smith*: Although many would say that the world is becoming a very ugly place, that life is hard, life is cruel, life is ugly.

*Rushforth*: It is also beautiful, it is also very beautiful, it needn't be ugly.

*Smith*: In what way would you say it is beautiful?

*Rushforth*: Well the children are so beautiful and the children's laughter is beautiful and the children's little ways are beautiful. But it is not only the children. I have people coming here whose lives are beautiful, very beautiful. I have people and I see their lives changing from sorrow to happiness. I think that there must be something that we think of almost as leaven, as yeast, that is working in this world, this ugly world, and that this beauty is wherever the yeast grains touch down, wherever they spread, something is happening.

*Smith*: But do you never look back over the years with some yearning to what was and has now gone?

*Rushforth*: No. I believe that all through life something is always happening, something is always coming to itself and this is a by-word in my life, '*something is happening*'. I am writing a book or have written a book that is waiting to be put together by the publisher and the publisher has chosen its name. He says it is to be called 'Something Is Happening'.

*Smith*: What would you most like people to value in you?

*Rushforth*: In me? Oh just me! I think that it is very important not to think it is one's teaching: one's teaching may go out of date.

*Smith*: You have kindly been answering questions that I have been putting to you about yourself, How have you felt about answering those questions?

*Rushforth*: Sometimes a bit puzzled, but quite glad that you should ask me the questions. It is quite good to think again about one's own life and perhaps when people hear what you are going to tell them about me they may say 'her life is worthwhile, I wonder if our lives too can be worthwhile, what's her secret?'

*Smith*: And what is the secret?

*Rushforth*: I say I was born of good parents. What's your secret? I always sleep with my window wide open summer and winter! What's your secret? What is *the* secret? I think the secret is the practise of the presence of God, seeking to plug in, to be in contact with That; That, which is so much more than oneself.

*(April, 1980)*